T0163723

MemoryBanc

Praise for

MemoryBanc®

YOUR WORKBOOK FOR ORGANIZING LIFE

"If only we had Kay Bransford's comprehensive MemoryBanc workbook when my wife and I were caring for our aging parents. We'll be using it to make sure our kids have everything they need to know in one place."

—**Bart Astor**, author of the best-selling *AARP Roadmap for the Rest of Your Life*

"MemoryBanc is an indispensable tool for insuring that the critical information we need to pass on to our family, friends, and others is organized, easily accessible, and clear. Kay Bransford has meticulously created a way to keep all those passwords, bank account data, legal information, and all that other stuff we never remember to share in one simple place. I tell all my clients to get it and fill it out—someone will definitely thank you for doing it!"

—**Cynthia R. Green**, Ph.D., founder and lead trainer, Total Brain Health

"Everybody in the world needs to own a copy of this book. MemoryBanc provides an incredibly comprehensive approach to making sure all the important details of your life are compiled and available if you need them. It's great for your aging parents; it's great for anyone. As I went through it page by page, I realized how much this book would help me to organize my life. And to help someone else in the event they needed to step in and help me. The caregiver's personal assistant!"

—**Gary McClain**, Ph.D., founder, Just Got Diagnosed

"What a great resource! This workbook provides useful forms, strategies, and tips for organizing important information for all generations. This process can be overwhelming, but MemoryBanc streamlines the gathering of all the pieces."

—**Barbara McVicker**, eldercare expert and host of the
PBS TV special *Stuck in the Middle: Caring for Mom and Dad*

MemoryBanc®
YOUR WORKBOOK FOR ORGANIZING LIFE

KAY H. BRANSFORD

New York

MemoryBanc®
YOUR WORKBOOK FOR ORGANIZING LIFE

© 2015 KAY H. BRANSFORD.

All rights reserved. No portion of this book may be reproduced, stored in a retrieval system, or transmitted in any form or by any means—electronic, mechanical, photocopy, recording, scanning, or other,—except for brief quotations in critical reviews or articles, without the prior written permission of the publisher.

Published in New York, New York, by Morgan James Publishing. Morgan James and The Entrepreneurial Publisher are trademarks of Morgan James, LLC.
www.MorganJamesPublishing.com

The Morgan James Speakers Group can bring authors to your live event. For more information or to book an event visit The Morgan James Speakers Group at
www.TheMorganJamesSpeakersGroup.com.

MemoryBanc® Your Workbook for Organizing Life ("workbook") was developed over the course of five years to identify, collect, and manage personal information, including financial, medical, online, and household details. It incorporates feedback from hundreds of clients, estate lawyers, financial advisors, and professional organizers. The stories shared are related to the author's personal experiences and should not be construed as professional advice.

Limit of Liability/Disclaimer of Warranty: While the publisher and the author have used their best efforts in preparing this workbook, they make no representations or warranties with respect to the accuracy or completeness of the contents of this workbook and specifically disclaim any implied warranties of merchantability or fitness for a particular purpose. No warranty may be created or extended by sales representatives or written sales materials. The advice and strategies contained herein may not be suitable for your situation. You should consult with a professional where appropriate. If professional assistance is required, the services of a competent professional person should be sought. The publisher and the author shall not be liable for damages arising here from. The fact that an organization or website is referred to in this work as a citation and/or a potential source of further information does not mean that the author or the publisher endorse the information that the organization or website may provide or recommendations it may make. Further, readers should be aware that websites listed in this work may have changed or disappeared between when this was written and when it is read.

A **free** eBook edition is available
with the purchase of this print book.

CLEARLY PRINT YOUR NAME ABOVE IN UPPER CASE

Instructions to claim your free eBook edition:
1. Download the BitLit app for Android or iOS
2. Write your name in **UPPER CASE** on the line
3. Use the BitLit app to submit a photo
4. Download your eBook to any device

ISBN 978-1-63047-249-8 paperback
ISBN 978-1-63047-250-4 eBook
Library of Congress Control Number:
2014938444

Cover Design by:
Paul McCarthy

Interior Design by:
Bonnie Bushman
bonnie@caboodlegraphics.com

In an effort to support local communities, raise awareness and funds, Morgan James Publishing donates a percentage of all book sales for the life of each book to Habitat for Humanity Peninsula and Greater Williamsburg.

Get involved today, visit
www.MorganJamesBuilds.com

Habitat
for Humanity®
Peninsula and
Greater Williamsburg
Building Partner

Dedication

To my mom and dad, who gave me so much and unknowingly inspired me to create this workbook, and to my husband and children, who helped me manage as I was living through the very reasons completing each page was important.

Table of Contents

Introduction

We all know that we should plan for future life-changing events, but it's one of the first things we put on the back burner. We have a million excuses, and have learned that procrastination doesn't work, but there are some things we just never make time to complete.

When it comes to organizing your personal information, doing it later is often too late. The statistics are alarming—some 43 percent of all people age 40 now will have a long-term disability event prior to reaching age 65. And seven out of ten people who turn 65 today will need some type of long-term care services and support lasting three or more years. Could a loved one act as your medical advocate and provide your medical history or list of medications if you were unable to? Could someone else access your bill-paying account to cover basic expenses while you recovered?

The first edition of this workbook was designed in an effort to help caregivers, but within the first year of release most owners reported using it to organize their own households. Most of the ways we manage information and personal details come from a world where paper and mail ruled. Today, most Americans manage more than 28 online accounts; pay bills electronically; and store the details of their lives in their heads, on their phones and computers, and in the cloud. When the information is needed, it's difficult to find. Should your loved ones ever need it, they may never be able to find it, or if they can, access it.

Individuals in joint households report they "divide and conquer" their financial and household tasks. If a partner was suddenly incapacitated, many realize they'd be up the proverbial creek and unable to manage what their partner had been doing. And if you live on your own, it's doubtful that friends or family would know the details of your life and your wishes if they wanted to help you.

For all these reasons, this workbook is important. You will be able to document your life details and put them in a format that will make it easier for you to retrieve and for someone else to access if you're not able to handle matters on your own. This workbook will walk you through the process of identifying and documenting those details in a way that makes it easy for you to organize your accounts, and for someone else to step in and help you—even if only temporarily—should you need it.

MemoryBanc won the 2013 AARP Foundation Prize for Older-Adult Focused Innovation.

CHAPTER 1

How to Use MemoryBanc to Fight Information Overload

We are bombarded and overwhelmed with information. What used to only come in the mail now also arrives by email, text, and phone. The roster of personal papers we used to keep in a file cabinet or in our safe now includes account numbers, usernames, passcodes, PINs, and security questions we have stored in our heads, under our keyboards, and on our mobile devices.

When asked, we don't always know where to find our own information. We might be surprised to learn how much of our information is stored digitally, but usually only notice when the power is out, our computer crashes, or a website is down.

Then there's the problem of who knows what. Whether you live on your own or with family members, you may manage only a portion of your financial and household responsibilities. In many homes, management is divided among various people.

Of course, you still need to consult professionals to assist with your estate and financial planning. But this workbook will help you organize the financial, health, and other important details of your life. Having easily accessible information from your bank accounts to medical records will help you and your family retrieve this data quickly and easily when it is needed.

This workbook contains a variety of worksheets to help you organize, record, and protect your information, accounts, documents, usernames, and passcodes. Complete the worksheets and store a copy at home, in a place you and your loved ones can access. You can make copies, write in pencil, and reuse pages as information changes.

If you'd prefer a more portable and paperless organization system, you can order a flash drive that arrives preloaded with MemoryBanc pages in an editable PDF format so you can add, edit, and store your information digitally. It comes with 2 GB of space, enough to include estate papers, personal documents, and photos—any files you would like to secure. To learn more about this option, visit the registration/order discount form in the back of this workbook or our website at www.MemoryBanc.com.

Five Steps to Collecting and Compiling Personal Details

Filling out this workbook the first time requires your careful attention. The completed worksheets should be reviewed at least once a year since this information changes over time.

Step One: Review the MemoryBanc

To begin, review each section of the workbook and inventory the information you will need.

Step Two: Collect the Data

Collect the information so you are ready to fill out this workbook. If you are not organized, it may take some time to locate all the information—all the more reason to complete this workbook. This will be the last time you need to go on this type of scavenger hunt.

Step Three: Complete the Worksheets

You can now fill out the workbook. Don't feel like you have to tackle it all in one sitting. Set up several 15-minute or half-hour appointments with yourself or your loved ones. Most people find that two or three appointments will be enough time to get the bulk of the workbook completed.

Follow the prompts and complete each section. We recommend you have Post-it notes on hand to flag missing information so you can easily return to complete a section.

If you are completing this workbook for multiple members of a household, use the field "Name" at the top of the worksheets to designate the person to which the information applies. Likewise, for the worksheets related to a physical location, use the field "Service Address" at the top.

Step Four: Store and Share This Information

Find a safe place to store your workbook and make sure that you share its location with those individuals who would step in to help, should you ever need it.

For safekeeping, we recommend you make a copy of the completed pages and keep them in a secure location. Many families have given a copy of their completed forms to a loved one, so in an emergency, the person you choose to step in to help you would have all the information he/she would need. Include copies of your medical directives, durable power of attorney, will, and trust if you have them.

Step Five: Set Up Regular Review Periods

This is not a process you do once and never look at again. You will add and change financial services providers, continue to accumulate medical history, sign up for new online accounts, or purchase a new home, car, and appliances. Use the schedule on page four to record your updates as you make them.

At a minimum, you should review this workbook annually. We also recommend reviewing it if you experience any major life changes such as a move, job change, death of a loved one, and health concern.

Update Schedule

Name _____

Keeping Your Information Up to Date

Use this schedule to keep track of the updates you have made to your workbook. As mentioned, we recommend you review it at least once a year to keep it current.

Section	Date of completion or last update with initials
Personal	
Cash Flow	
Financial	
Online/Internet	
Medical	
Household	
Birthdays and Anniversaries	
Contacts	
Frequent Flyer Accounts	
Pet/Pet Care	
Schedules	
Subscriptions/Memberships	

_____

_____

_____

_____

_____

©2015 MemoryBanc

CHAPTER 2

Personal Section

Starting at the Top: Documenting Personal Record Details and Locations

If you have ever had to support a loved one as a caregiver and managed their personal accounts, you are aware of the number of documents and details you will be asked to provide. This section will prompt you through the process of collecting and documenting the basic details about you and your spouse, children, beneficiaries, and key contacts. It also features a quick locator for crucial personal documents.

Some of the steps will help you in the event you lose or misplace a purse or wallet or are applying for a loan, and other steps will help should a loved one ever need to step in and assist you.

In 2014, *Consumer Reports* noted that 29 percent of online consumers' home computers were infected by malicious software. For this reason, we recommend you do not store any of your confidential information on your computer unless you are using proven encryption software. That encryption software, however, might also prevent your loved ones from accessing information they may need if you are incapacitated.

In addition to completing these pages, make color copies of the items in your wallet as well as copies of other key documents. You'll want to include these:

- Driver's license
- Credit cards
- Social Security card
- Military identification card
- Passport
- Immigration or citizenship papers
- Birth certificate
- Adoption papers
- Marriage certificates and prenuptial agreements
- Divorce or separation papers
- Service records (especially your DD214)
- Professional license numbers and/or educational transcripts that would be required to claim specific benefits for services

There are a variety of instances where you might be asked to provide copies of these documents. As an executor, I needed to provide a color copy of my father's driver's license, his service records, and marriage certificate as well as his death certificate to claim benefits and transition accounts into my mother's name. Having these documents already organized made handling these matters simple.

If you have a home safe, specify the location with instructions on how to open your safe. If you have a bank safe deposit box, you will need to set up signatory access in advance as well as leave an address and key.

Storing your documents in a bank safe deposit box that your loved ones cannot access may make it very difficult for them to retrieve needed documents when they need them. For those with a durable power of attorney and medical directives, if the only copies reside in your bank box, how could they be used when they might be needed? For those who have their will stored in a bank box, it could be very difficult to access after your death. In Virginia, if you die and no one has signatory access, your loved ones will have to present a death certificate, and a sheriff is called. If your relatives cannot produce the key, the bank will call a special locksmith, and your family will bear the cost of drilling and replacing the drilled box.

The reality is that someone will need to step in and assist you before you die. Instead of storing your critical documents in a bank safe deposit box, consider a fire- and water-resistant safe. *Consumer Reports* recommends getting a safe with at least 30 minutes of protection from fire. If you do not live in a major metropolitan area, or want to store film, digital media, or sensitive papers, you should contact a reputable, safe firm for a recommendation.

Name _____

Personal Profile

	Name	Social Security number	Birth date
Self	_____	_____-_____-_____	____/____/____
Spouse	_____	_____-_____-_____	____/____/____
Children	_____	_____-_____-_____	____/____/____
	_____	_____-_____-_____	____/____/____
	_____	_____-_____-_____	____/____/____
	_____	_____-_____-_____	____/____/____
	_____	_____-_____-_____	____/____/____
	_____	_____-_____-_____	____/____/____

OTHER BENEFICIARIES

_____	_____-_____-_____	____/____/____
_____	_____-_____-_____	____/____/____

CONTACT INFORMATION

Home address _____

City _____ State _____ ZIP_____

Home phone (_____) _____ Cell (_____) _____

Email _____

Business address_____

City _____ State _____ ZIP_____

Business phone (_____) _____ Business cell (_____) _____

Business email _____

Key Contacts and Advisors

FINANCIAL ADVISOR

Name/Company _____

Phone (_____) _____ Email _____

Address_____

Related documents held by financial advisor _____

My copies of documents and materials are stored _____

ATTORNEY

Name/Company _____

Phone (_____) _____ Email _____

Address_____

Related documents held by attorney _____

My copies of documents and materials are stored _____

ACCOUNTANT

Name/Company _____

Phone (_____) _____ Email _____

Address_____

Related documents held by accountant _____

My copies of documents and materials are stored _____

INSURANCE AGENT

Name/Company _____

Phone (_____) _____ Email _____

Address_____

Related documents held by insurance agent _____

My copies of documents and materials are stored _____

©2015 MemoryBanc

Name _____

Key Contacts and Advisors (cont.)

PERSONAL REPRESENTATIVE/EXECUTOR

Name/Company _____

Phone (_____) _____ Email _____

Address_____

Related documents held by representative _____

My copies of documents and materials are stored _____

SPIRITUAL/CLERGY

Name/Company _____

Phone (_____) _____ Email _____

Address_____

Related documents held by spiritual/clergy member _____

My copies of documents and materials are stored _____

OTHER

Name/Company _____

Phone (_____) _____ Email _____

Address_____

Related documents held by other _____

My copies of documents and materials are stored _____

GUARDIAN/TRUSTEE

In the event I become incapacitated or am disabled and unable to manage my own affairs, I have named this person (other than a spouse) to act as my guardian or trustee:

Name/Company _____

Phone (_____) _____ Email _____

Address_____

Please visit the Medical Section starting on page 81 to record doctors, dentists, therapists, and other individuals related to your healthcare.

Location of Important Personal Documents

	Last Updated	Location
Adoption papers	Not applicable	_____
Birth certificate(s)	Not applicable	_____
Burial instructions and papers	___ / ___ / ___	_____
Citizenship/ immigration papers	Not applicable	_____
Divorce documents	Not applicable	_____
Durable power of attorney	___ / ___ / ___	_____
Household deed(s)/ land record(s)	___ / ___ / ___	_____
Household inventory	___ / ___ / ___	_____
Life insurance	___ / ___ / ___	_____
Living will(s)/medical directive(s)	___ / ___ / ___	_____
Long-term care insurance	___ / ___ / ___	_____
Marriage certificate	Not applicable	_____
Military service records	___ / ___ / ___	_____
Social Security card(s)	Not applicable	_____
Trust(s)	___ / ___ / ___	_____
Will(s)	___ / ___ / ___	_____
Other _____	___ / ___ / ___	_____
Other _____	___ / ___ / ___	_____
Other _____	___ / ___ / ___	_____

©2015 MemoryBanc

Name _____

Location of Important Personal Documents (cont.)

Tax returns (years/location)_____
_____
_____
_____

Appraisals and/or inventory of collections _____
_____
_____
_____

Personal safe (location and combination) _____

Contents _____
_____
_____

Safe deposit box (location and number) _____

Address _____

Contact _____ Phone (_____) _____

Names of those authorized to open safe deposit box _____
_____

Location of key(s) _____

Contents _____
_____
_____
_____
_____

Licenses and Certifications

	Expiration	Number	Location
Driver's license	___/___/___	_____	_____
Driver's license	___/___/___	_____	_____
Passport	___/___/___	_____	_____
Passport	___/___/___	_____	_____
Other	___/___/___	_____	_____
Other	___/___/___	_____	_____
Other	___/___/___	_____	_____
Other	___/___/___	_____	_____

Additional related details or important information

_____

_____

_____

_____

_____

_____

_____

_____

_____

_____

_____

_____

©2015 MemoryBanc

Frequently Asked Questions about Organizing Personal Information

Q: Can I make copies of this workbook?

A: Once you have completed the forms, we hope you will share copies of the completed pages with those individuals who you trust. If you would prefer an expandable system that allows for easy updates, free refills, and additions, you should consider the MemoryBanc® Register™. The Register includes 8.5 x 11 inch preprinted workbook pages delivered in a three-ring leather-like binder and Personal, Financial, Medical, Online, Household, and Other section tabs. This edition can be tailored to meet your specific needs as your information changes, assets grow, and medical and online accounts accumulate. To learn more about this option, visit the registration/order discount form in the back of this workbook or our website at www.MemoryBanc.com.

Q: I would like to complete this workbook and give a copy to my son. I'm worried about burdening him with the task of being my advocate or executor. What have other families done?

A: Many families have avoided discussing how loved one's could help if a crisis strikes and because of it the library is filled with scores of books to help adult children who are thrust into a decision-making role and aren't prepared. The best thing to do is ask your child(ren). If you need some help getting the conversation started, check out *The Other Talk* by Tim Prosch, who offers practical advice and some communication tools to foster an open, honest discussion on this very subject.

Q: I gave this workbook to my mom, but she wasn't interested in sitting down with me to work on the content. How have others overcome their loved ones' resistance?

A: You won't be the first adult child who Mom or Dad has shooed out of the room when you bring up this topic. However, one of the best ways to start this conversation is to ask your parent(s) if you could count on them to be your backup, and share how you have documented your wishes using MemoryBanc and where your information is stored. You may need to revisit the topic a few times before they are ready to share information with you. Ideal times to work with them on the workbook include:

- When they ask you to be their executor or share their estate planning documents with you. Let them know you are honored to be asked and request that they schedule some time to sit with you to share the information you would need to fulfill this role.

- When something has happened to a family friend. This can be a good time to warmly ask how your parent might want you to help if your family was faced with a similar situation.

- At family gatherings when all siblings and/or children are together. You could ask where your parent has put information like a personal medical history or healthcare wishes to open up a conversation.

If a parent has cognitive impairment, there may never be a good time. It could be that the person doesn't remember much of the information and is afraid of you finding this out. In this case, you will have to focus on finding mailings and checking files to collect the information you need. A cell phone with a camera can be an easy way to gather information without Mom or Dad feeling as if you are taking over all their paperwork. In general, you will need to be patient, take it slow, and look for windows of opportunity to raise these issues. A useful resource if you have a loved one with a suspected cognitive impairment or a dementia diagnosis can be found at DealingwithDementia.org.

Q: As a parent of adult children, shouldn't I know what my kids expect if something were to happen to one of them?

A: Yes. If there is someone in your life that would turn to you for help, giving them a copy of this workbook is a positive way to let them know you would help, should they ever need it.

Q: How do I respond to Dad when he tells me his attorney or accountant has all of this information?

A: While the attorneys might have the documents, they typically don't have their clients' medical records, online passcodes, or personal contacts. Ask Dad if he expects that the attorney will be joining him on medical visits and paying bills. If not, suggest he speak with his attorney on how to ensure someone is able to help him, should it ever be needed.

Q: My mom named me on her durable power of attorney form—isn't that all I need to help her?

A: The durable power of attorney was the most important document I held that allowed me to help my parents when they were unable to act on their own behalf. Some institutions readily accepted it when I provided a copy, and I was quickly added to their accounts.

However, in several cases it was very difficult to use. Even though my state (Virginia) has a statute saying an institution is obligated to accept the document, one financial institution would not accept it because it was more than two years old and a second refused because it was more than five years old. Some institutions took several months to process it before I was granted the ability to make any changes to the account.

If you don't have a durable power of attorney, you can request and complete the "power of attorney" form from the specific financial institution. These forms are designed to allow account holders to define individuals and access rights. You will have to complete one from each institution for access, and these immediately take effect. But if someone is incapacitated, it will be too late to go this route. These documents require a notary to validate identification, and the signer will need to be alert and have decision-making capacity.

Q: My sister named me as executor in her will. What do I need to know?

A: The job of executor is an honor that includes a huge responsibility. It could require hours of work over several weeks and months, and it demands great attention to detail. If you have been asked to fulfill this role, we recommend, at a minimum, that you give her a copy of this workbook to document her estate. If she has also named you in her durable power of attorney, or on her healthcare directives, in addition to being sure to have a valid copy of the legal documents, ask her to review this workbook with you annually so you have what you need to fulfill this role.

CHAPTER 3

Financial Section

Creating a Treasure Map: Organizing Financial Records and Account Details

In 2013, *CNNMoney* reported that $58 billion in "missing money" was sitting with state and federal treasurers. This includes insurance policies, bank accounts, 401(k) plans, federal tax refunds, U.S. Treasury securities, and even physical assets lost in the shuffle of moves, personal crises, and death. The use of online credit and payment tools is only going to accelerate the contributions to this unclaimed money pool.

What many people don't realize is how quickly their financial information changes. Regularly updating the details makes it easier for you to access your accounts while providing a simple way to check that none of your money is lost in a move or personal crisis.

If you have gotten remarried or divorced, or have experienced the loss of a close family member, you should also review the named beneficiaries on your accounts.

One way to easily manage your accounts is to set up online access. You can easily initiate bill payments, access old bank and credit card statements, and even update services. While I held durable power of attorney for my parents, having online access to their accounts gave me the ability to easily and quickly help manage bill payments and household accounts.

A major timesaver is to include the credit card details on any accounts and services that automatically debit against your card. When a card is lost, compromised, or expired, you can easily update the accounts connected with that credit card.

If you own a small business and don't have these items documented or systems in place to manage without you, consider providing instructions on how to find these:

- Customer list/key customers
- Online accounts and access codes
- Incorporation documents
- Copyright/trademark records
- Business tax and insurance documents
- Intellectual property/non-compete agreements
- Vendor contracts, vendor contacts, and subscriptions
- Contact information or location of accounting and personnel records, along with access instructions

Many individuals are under the impression that your financial advisor, accountant, or tax preparer has this information. While these providers may be aware of your accounts and have access to some of them, you would need to agree to services and set up rights in advance. Without specific power of attorney rights, neither these professionals nor your loved ones will be able to use or reach this money on your behalf even if it was needed for your care, to pay your mortgage, or to continue your business until you recover.

For concerns about how to manage should you need help, we recommend you consult with an estate lawyer and financial advisor to find the solution that is right for you.

Name _____

Monthly Cash Flow

TOTAL ESTIMATED INCOME	$ _____
TOTAL ESTIMATED EXPENSES	$ _____
HOUSING	$ _____
AUTO/OTHER LOANS	$ _____
UTILITIES	$ _____
CREDIT CARDS	$ _____
HOUSEHOLD SERVICES	$ _____
OTHER	$ _____
NET MONTHLY CASH FLOW	$ _____

Last reviewed and updated

_____	_____
_____	_____
_____	_____
_____	_____
_____	_____
_____	_____
_____	_____

Income Summary

MONTHLY INCOME

Description/Source	$ Monthly/Pay date(s)	Notes

OTHER INCOME

Description/Source	$ Amount/Pay cycle	Notes

TOTAL ESTIMATED MONTHLY INCOME $ _____

©2015 MemoryBanc

Name _____

Expenses Summary

HOUSING

Description/Expense	Monthly/Quarterly/Annually (circle M/Q/A and list due date and $)	Notes
	M/Q/A $	
	M/Q/A $	
	M/Q/A $	

AUTO/OTHER LOANS

Description/Expense	Monthly/Quarterly/Annually (circle M/Q/A and list due date and $)	Notes
	M/Q/A $	
	M/Q/A $	
	M/Q/A $	
	M/Q/A $	
	M/Q/A $	

UTILITIES

Description/Expense	Monthly/Quarterly/Annually (circle M/Q/A and list due date and $)	Notes
	M/Q/A $	
	M/Q/A $	
	M/Q/A $	
	M/Q/A $	
	M/Q/A $	
	M/Q/A $	
	M/Q/A $	
	M/Q/A $	
	M/Q/A $	

CREDIT CARDS

Description/Expense	Monthly/Quarterly/Annually (circle M/Q/A and list due date and $)		Notes
	M/Q/A	$	
	M/Q/A	$	
	M/Q/A	$	
	M/Q/A	$	
	M/Q/A	$	

HOUSEHOLD SERVICES

Description/Expense	Monthly/Quarterly/Annually (circle M/Q/A and list due date and $)		Notes
	M/Q/A	$	
	M/Q/A	$	
	M/Q/A	$	
	M/Q/A	$	

OTHER (FOOD/INSURANCE/CLOTHING/MEMBERSHIPS/EDUCATION/MISCELLANEOUS)

Description/Expense	Monthly/Quarterly/Annually (circle M/Q/A and list due date and $)		Notes
	M/Q/A	$	
	M/Q/A	$	
	M/Q/A	$	
	M/Q/A	$	
	M/Q/A	$	
	M/Q/A	$	
	M/Q/A	$	

©2015 MemoryBanc

Name _____

Monthly/Quarterly/Annual Income

INCOME

Take-home pay, retirement, interest/dividends, alimony/child support, investments, etc.

Income source _____

Address _____

Contact name _____ Phone (_____) _____

Pay cycle _____ Monthly estimated income (after taxes) $_____

Notes _____

Income source _____

Address _____

Contact name _____ Phone (_____) _____

Pay cycle _____ Monthly estimated income (after taxes) $ _____

Notes _____

Income source _____

Address _____

Contact name _____ Phone (_____) _____

Pay cycle _____ Monthly estimated income (after taxes) $ _____

Notes _____

Additional related details or important information regarding these accounts

_____

_____

_____

_____

_____

_____

_____

© MemoryBanc 2015

Name _____

Bank and Investment Accounts

Bank/Institution _____

Address _____

Title (names) on account _____

Contact name _____

Phone (_____) _____ Email _____

Website _____ PIN _____

Username _____ Passcode _____

- Account number _____ Type of account _____

  Notes _____

- Account number _____ Type of account _____

  Notes _____

Bank/Institution _____

Address _____

Title (names) on account _____

Contact name _____

Phone (_____) _____ Email _____

Website _____ PIN _____

Username _____ Passcode _____

- Account number _____ Type of account _____

  Notes _____

- Account number _____ Type of account _____

  Notes _____

Bank and Investment Accounts (cont.)

Bank/Institution _____

Address _____

Title (names) on account _____

Contact name _____

Phone (_____) _____ Email _____

Website _____ PIN _____

Username _____ Passcode _____

- Account number _____ Type of account _____

  Notes _____

- Account number _____ Type of account _____

  Notes _____

Bank/Institution _____

Address _____

Title (names) on account _____

Contact name _____

Phone (_____) _____ Email _____

Website _____ PIN _____

Username _____ Passcode _____

- Account number _____ Type of account _____

  Notes _____

- Account number _____ Type of account _____

  Notes _____

©2015 MemoryBanc

Name _____

Trust Accounts/Securities

TRUST ACCOUNTS

Institution _____ Type of trust _____

Address_____

Tax ID number _____ Current trustee(s) _____

Successor trustee _____

Beneficiaries _____

Notes _____

Institution _____ Type of trust _____

Address_____

Tax ID number _____ Current trustee(s) _____

Successor trustee _____

Beneficiaries _____

Notes _____

SECURITIES

Brokerage firm _____ Account number _____

Title (names) on account _____ Type of account _____

Website _____ PIN _____

Username _____ Passcode _____

Notes _____

Brokerage firm _____ Account number _____

Title (names) on account _____ Type of account _____

Website _____ PIN _____

Username _____ Passcode _____

Notes _____

© MemoryBanc 2015

Name _____

IRAs/Retirement Accounts

Type _____

Participant _____

Company/Contact _____ Phone (_____) _____

Address _____

Account number _____ Approximate value $ _____

Primary beneficiaries _____

Contingent beneficiaries _____

Website _____ PIN _____

Username _____ Passcode _____

Type _____

Participant _____

Company/Contact _____ Phone (_____) _____

Address _____

Account number _____ Approximate value $ _____

Primary beneficiaries _____

Contingent beneficiaries _____

Website _____ PIN _____

Username _____ Passcode _____

Additional related details or important information regarding these accounts

_____

_____

_____

_____

_____

_____

_____

_____

Type _____

Participant _____

Company/Contact _____ Phone (_____) _____

Address _____

Account number _____ Approximate value $ _____

Primary beneficiaries _____

Contingent beneficiaries _____

Website _____ PIN _____

Username _____ Passcode _____

Type _____

Participant _____

Company/Contact _____ Phone (_____) _____

Address _____

Account number _____ Approximate value $ _____

Primary beneficiaries _____

Contingent beneficiaries _____

Website _____ PIN _____

Username _____ Passcode _____

Additional related details or important information regarding these accounts

_____

_____

_____

_____

_____

_____

©2015 MemoryBanc

Name _____

Insurance Policies

HOME/RENTAL

Owned by _____ Type of policy _____

Policy number _____ Issuer _____

Contact _____ Phone (_____) _____

Replacement coverage_____

Coverage limits _____

Annual premium $ _____ Annual renewal date _____ / _____
                                                    (MM)   (DD)

Website _____ PIN _____

Username _____ Passcode _____

LIFE

Owned by _____ Type of policy _____

Policy number _____ Issuer _____

Contact _____ Phone (_____) _____

Beneficiary(ies) _____

Death benefit $ _____ Cash value $ _____

Annual premium $ _____ Annual renewal date _____ / _____
                                                    (MM)   (DD)

Website _____ PIN _____

Username _____ Passcode _____

Please visit the Medical Section to record health,
supplemental, and long-term care insurance.

Insurance Policies (cont.)

AUTO

Issuer/contact _____ Policy number _____

Address _____ Phone (_____) _____

Drivers insured_____

• Year/Make/Model _____ License plate _____

• Year/Make/Model _____ License plate _____

• Year/Make/Model _____ License plate _____

Annual premium $ _____ Annual renewal date _____ /_____

                                                   (MM)   (DD)

Website _____ PIN _____

Username _____ Passcode _____

OTHER _____

Covers _____

Owned by _____ Type of policy _____

Policy number _____ Issuer _____

Contact _____ Phone (_____) _____

Beneficiary(ies) _____

Notes _____

Annual premium $ _____ Annual renewal date _____ /_____

                                                   (MM)   (DD)

Website _____ PIN _____

Username _____ Passcode _____

©2015 MemoryBanc

Name _____

Real Estate

HOUSING/PROPERTY/REAL ESTATE LOANS

Type of ownership: Full/Partial interest/Other _____

Location of property _____

Initial purchase price _____ Purchase date _____

Lender _____ Account number _____

Lender's address _____

Loan amount $_____ Monthly payment amount $_____

Property improvement details _____

_____

Related fees (homeowner association or condominium fees) $ _____

Location of related records _____

RENTAL/RENTER

Property address _____

Landlord/Renter _____ Account number _____

Landlord's address _____

Landlord/Renter phone (_____) _____ Term of agreement _____

Monthly payment amount $ _____ Monthly billing due date _____

Related fees (homeowner association or condominium fees) $_____

Special notes related to property_____

_____

Additional related details or important information regarding these properties

_____

_____

_____

Other Investments/Asset Details

ANNUITIES

Owned by	Account type	Issuer	Beneficiary	Death benefit	Cash value
				$	$
				$	$
				$	$
				$	$

Additional related details or important information regarding these accounts

_____

COLLECTIONS

Description _____

Location of collection _____

Inventory _____

Additional details _____

Description _____

Location of collection _____

Inventory _____

Additional details _____

Description _____

Location of collection _____

Inventory _____

Additional details _____

©2015 MemoryBanc

Name _____

Vehicle Loans

AUTO LOANS

Year/Make/Model _____ Location _____

Lender _____ Lender's address _____

Account number _____ Loan amount $ _____

Payment amount $ _____ Monthly billing due date _____

Additional details _____

Year/Make/Model _____ Location _____

Lender _____ Lender's address _____

Account number _____ Loan amount $ _____

Payment amount $ _____ Monthly billing due date _____

Additional details _____

Year/Make/Model _____ Location _____

Lender _____ Lender's address _____

Account number _____ Loan amount $ _____

Payment amount $ _____ Monthly billing due date _____

Additional details _____

Additional related details or important information regarding these accounts

_____

_____

_____

_____

_____

_____

_____

OTHER LOAN (not home or auto loan)

Loan description _____

Lender _____ Lender's address _____

Account number _____ Loan amount $ _____

Payment amount $ _____ Monthly billing due date _____

Additional details _____

OTHER LOAN (not home or auto loan)

Loan description _____

Lender _____ Lender's address _____

Account number _____ Loan amount $ _____

Payment amount $ _____ Monthly billing due date _____

Additional details _____

OTHER LOAN (not home or auto loan)

Loan description _____

Lender _____ Lender's address _____

Account number _____ Loan amount $ _____

Payment amount $ _____ Monthly billing due date _____

Additional details _____

Additional related details or important information regarding these accounts

_____

_____

_____

_____

_____

_____

©2015 MemoryBanc

Name _____

Credit Cards

CREDIT CARDS (BANK AND RETAIL CARDS)

Card name _____ Card number _____

Card issuer address _____

Exp. date _____ Security code _____ Monthly billing due date _____

Phone (_____) _____

Website _____ PIN _____

Username_____ Passcode _____

Auto-payment card use (list linked account(s) and related payment date(s)) _____

_____

_____

_____

Card name _____ Card number _____

Card issuer address _____

Exp. date _____ Security code _____ Monthly billing due date _____

Phone (_____) _____

Website _____ PIN _____

Username_____ Passcode _____

Auto-payment card use (list linked account(s) and related payment date(s)) _____

_____

_____

_____

Credit Cards (cont.)

Card name _____ Card number _____

Card issuer address _____

Exp. date _____ Security code _____ Monthly billing due date _____

Phone (_____) _____

Website _____ PIN _____

Username _____ Passcode _____

Auto-payment card use (list linked account(s) and related payment date(s)) _____

_____

_____

_____

Card name _____ Card number _____

Card issuer address _____

Exp. date _____ Security code _____ Monthly billing due date _____

Phone (_____) _____

Website _____ PIN _____

Username _____ Passcode _____

Auto-payment card use (list linked account(s) and related payment date(s)) _____

_____

_____

_____

©2015 MemoryBanc

Name _____

Credit Cards

CREDIT CARDS (BANK AND RETAIL CARDS)

Card name _____ Card number _____

Card issuer address _____

Exp. date _____ Security code _____ Monthly billing due date _____

Phone (_____) _____

Website _____ PIN _____

Username _____ Passcode _____

Auto-payment card use (list linked account(s) and related payment date(s)) _____

_____

_____

_____

Card name _____ Card number _____

Card issuer address _____

Exp. date _____ Security code _____ Monthly billing due date _____

Phone (_____) _____

Website _____ PIN _____

Username _____ Passcode _____

Auto-payment card use (list linked account(s) and related payment date(s)) _____

_____

_____

_____

Card name _____ Card number _____

Card issuer address _____

Exp. date _____ Security code _____ Monthly billing due date _____

Phone (_____) _____

Website _____ PIN _____

Username_____ Passcode _____

Auto-payment card use (list linked account(s) and related payment date(s)) _____

_____

_____

_____

Card name _____ Card number _____

Card issuer address _____

Exp. date _____ Security code _____ Monthly billing due date _____

Phone (_____) _____

Website _____ PIN _____

Username_____ Passcode _____

Auto-payment card use (list linked account(s) and related payment date(s)) _____

_____

_____

_____

©2015 MemoryBanc

Name _____

Credit Cards

CREDIT CARDS (BANK AND RETAIL CARDS)

Card name _____ Card number _____

Card issuer address _____

Exp. date _____ Security code _____ Monthly billing due date _____

Phone (_____) _____

Website _____ PIN _____

Username_____ Passcode _____

Auto-payment card use (list linked account(s) and related payment date(s)) _____

_____

_____

_____

Card name _____ Card number _____

Card issuer address _____

Exp. date _____ Security code _____ Monthly billing due date _____

Phone (_____) _____

Website _____ PIN _____

Username_____ Passcode _____

Auto-payment card use (list linked account(s) and related payment date(s)) _____

_____

_____

_____

Credit Cards (cont.)

Card name _____ Card number _____

Card issuer address _____

Exp. date _____ Security code _____ Monthly billing due date _____

Phone (_____) _____

Website _____ PIN _____

Username _____ Passcode _____

Auto-payment card use (list linked account(s) and related payment date(s)) _____

_____

_____

_____

Card name _____ Card number _____

Card issuer address _____

Exp. date _____ Security code _____ Monthly billing due date _____

Phone (_____) _____

Website _____ PIN _____

Username _____ Passcode _____

Auto-payment card use (list linked account(s) and related payment date(s)) _____

_____

_____

_____

©2015 MemoryBanc

Service Address _____

Utilities

ELECTRIC

Provider name _____ Phone (_____) _____

Provider address _____

Account holder _____ Account number _____

Billing due date _____ (Monthly/Quarterly/Annually)

Website _____ PIN _____

Username _____ Passcode _____

Auto-payment information (list any linked payment account(s) and related payment date(s))

_____

_____

GAS

Provider name _____ Phone (_____) _____

Provider address _____

Account holder _____ Account number _____

Billing due date _____ (Monthly/Quarterly/Annually)

Website _____ PIN _____

Username _____ Passcode _____

Auto-payment information (list any linked payment account(s) and related payment date(s))

_____

_____

WATER

Provider name _____ Phone (_____) _____

Provider address _____

Account holder _____ Account number _____

Billing due date _____ (Monthly/Quarterly/Annually)

Website _____ PIN _____

Username _____ Passcode _____

Auto-payment information (list any linked payment account(s) and related payment date(s))

_____

_____

SEWER

Provider name _____ Phone (_____) _____

Provider address _____

Account holder _____ Account number _____

Billing due date _____ (Monthly/Quarterly/Annually)

Website _____ PIN _____

Username _____ Passcode _____

Auto-payment information (list any linked payment account(s) and related payment date(s))

_____

_____

©2015 MemoryBanc

Service Address _____

Utilities (cont.)

PHONE (Home/Mobile)

Provider name _____ Phone (_____) _____

Provider address _____

Account holder _____ Account number _____

Billing due date _____ (Monthly/Quarterly/Annually)

Website _____ PIN _____

Username _____ Passcode _____

Auto-payment information (list any linked payment account(s) and related payment date(s))

_____

_____

PHONE (Home/Mobile)

Provider name _____ Phone (_____) _____

Provider address _____

Account holder _____ Account number _____

Billing due date _____ (Monthly/Quarterly/Annually)

Website _____ PIN _____

Username _____ Passcode _____

Auto-payment information (list any linked payment account(s) and related payment date(s))

_____

_____

TRASH

Provider name _____ Phone (_____) _____

Provider address _____

Account holder _____ Account number _____

Billing due date _____ (Monthly/Quarterly/Annually)

Website _____ PIN _____

Username _____ Passcode _____

Auto-payment information (list any linked payment account(s) and related payment date(s))

_____

_____

INTERNET/CABLE/DISH

Provider name _____ Phone (_____) _____

Provider address _____

Account holder _____ Account number _____

Billing due date _____ (Monthly/Quarterly/Annually)

Website _____ PIN _____

Username _____ Passcode _____

Auto-payment information (list any linked payment account(s) and related payment date(s))

_____

_____

          ©2015 MemoryBanc

Service Address _____

Utilities (cont.)

OTHER _____

Provider name _____ Phone (_____) _____

Provider address _____

Account holder _____ Account number _____

Billing due date _____ (Monthly/Quarterly/Annually)

Website _____ PIN _____

Username _____ Passcode _____

Auto-payment information (list any linked payment account(s) and related payment date(s))

_____

_____

OTHER _____

Provider name _____ Phone (_____) _____

Provider address _____

Account holder _____ Account number _____

Billing due date _____ (Monthly/Quarterly/Annually)

Website _____ PIN _____

Username _____ Passcode _____

Auto-payment information (list any linked payment account(s) and related payment date(s))

_____

_____

Frequently Asked Questions about Banking and Financial Accounts

Q: My partner and I have a joint bank account, and I pay the bills. Won't my partner be able to use the bill payment I set up from his online access account?

A: That seems logical, but online bank accounts only display payee information to the account holder that established the payment account. Take time to check out your online bill pay solution and bank account. You will find that only the individual who set up the online bill pay vendor can see that account or make changes to it. You would be able to see the payment in your check register and monthly statement but unable to make changes to any automated payments that were set up under the joint account holder's login.

Q: We have "payable on death" accounts with our bank. Why is documenting this information important?

A: The reality of life is that most of us don't just die—we face illnesses and can even be incapacitated to the point that we can't act on our own behalf. Consult with an estate lawyer to ensure that your plan will work for you and your loved ones.

Q: I'm not a computer user, but I see you include prompts for usernames and passcodes. Can I just ignore that?

A: Online access made it easy for me to continue to pay my parents' bills when some of their financial institutions refused to accept their durable power of attorney. Online access also saved me time when dealing with their household accounts, such as their telephone and utilities. If the person who would help you is not in the area, or if you can sit with them in advance to review accounts and set up access, their job will be much easier if they ever need to step in and help you.

My parents wanted me to access and manage the accounts on their behalf, so my dad worked with me to create online access. This is something I suggest you and your loved ones consider setting up before you might need it.

Q: I set up all my passcodes in an app on my phone and shared the data with my spouse and my executor as key contacts. Won't that be enough?

A: The most popular solutions use encrypted data, which means if a passcode is lost or forgotten, the data can't be accessed. Encrypted data is a requirement for these solutions but not designed to make data portable when a loved one might need to access it. We recommend you store this information with your account details in the workbook and keep it, or a copy, in a safe place your loved ones or executor can access.

Q: I'm not married and I don't have children. Do I need to worry about documenting my accounts and details?

A: If you don't have someone who is familiar with your personal wishes as well as your general affairs, including your household bills, medical history, and online activities, it's vital that you document and set up loved ones who could assist you. If something were to happen to you, there are close friends and family that would want to help. Completing this workbook and talking to an estate lawyer will ensure those around you can step in to help, should you ever need it.

CHAPTER 4

Online Section

Taming the Internet:
Keeping Track of Online Passcodes

We manage, on average, more than two dozen accounts and passcodes, according to the credit scoring firm Experian. Documenting and updating usernames and passcodes in one secure place will make managing information easier and will save you time.

According to the Pew Research Center, 61 percent of Internet users in the United States bank online, 72 percent use social media, and 80 percent have shopped online. Those accounts make up your digital assets and include email accounts, social media, digital photos, music, movies, and e-books you've purchased.

Most of us immediately click "agree" when faced with terms of usage agreements, and with most online agreements, you will find that upon death, account rights cease and the account is not transferrable.

A *Wall Street Journal* story from 2013 titled "Life and Death Online: Who Controls a Digital Legacy?" brings light to this complicated issue. In this case, parents were unable to get access to their deceased 16-year-old daughter's online pictures and poetry. Most parents are unaware that they don't have rights to access their minors' accounts. The user agreements state that as a user, you agree to the conditions that the provider has defined.

We recommend that those of you with children under 18 have them document their usernames and passcodes. While my youngest and I sat together to set up her accounts so I could record her usernames and passcodes, I asked my son to just document and store his in a sealed envelope that I hope I never have to open.

Today, with many people using "the cloud" to store personal documents and photographs, it's even more important that you make available the keys to access these accounts with family and loved ones. Some of the most crucial data to record include your usernames, passcodes, PINs, and security questions.

Online access goes beyond email and social media. From your health insurance provider and online banking to your utility accounts, you will find that you can document those access codes with each of those records within this workbook.

To learn about creating secure passcodes, you should read AARP's *Protecting Yourself Online for Dummies* by Nancy Muir and Ryan Williams.

In addition to listing pertinent websites, URLs, usernames, passcodes, PINs, and security questions and answers, you should also list any linked credit cards. If a credit card is lost, compromised, or expires, you have an easy way to update payment methods for those accounts.

Are Online Assets Safe?

In August 2014, the *New York Times* reported that a Russian crime ring had stolen over 1.2 billion username and passcode combos and more than 500 million email addresses from some 420,000 websites. Add to that the increasing number of data breaches recently (Target, Michaels, and Nordstrom to name just a few), you should be wary of putting any of your sensitive personal information in a cloud-based storage application without at least encrypting the file first. The encryption, however, may make it impossible for even you to retrieve. If you want to store this information digitally, my recommendation is to store your personal accounts, papers, and details on a removable storage device—and keep it in a secure location.

Why Online Access Is Essential

Online access saved me hours of time when I needed to step in and manage my parents' affairs. Even mundane situations can arise that would require you to know the basics of your accounts. For example, if your spouse or partner were unavailable, would you be able to make changes to your mobile account or request service for an item under warranty? Many of these accounts include PINs or security questions.

Documenting the PINs, passcodes, and even security questions is essential so that your partner could use them to manage your shared lives, even if for only a temporary basis.

According to the FBI, the average burglar spends between eight and twelve minutes in your home and is looking for items that are easy to sell at a pawn shop such as electronics, gold, guns, jewelry, and silver, not a list of accounts and passcodes. You need to find the solution that will work for you and your loved ones.

Name _____

Security Questions

What is your mother's maiden name? _____

What is your father's first name? _____

What is your grandmother's maiden name? _____

What is your favorite

    food? _____

    movie? _____

    book? _____

What is the name of the town where you were born? _____

What is the name of your first pet? _____

What is the name of your favorite pet? _____

What is the make of your first car? _____

What was your childhood nickname? _____

What is the name of the town where your parents met? _____

What is the name of the city in which you met your spouse or partner?

_____

Use these to document additional security questions (Q) and answers (A):

Q: _____

    A: _____

Q: _____

    A: _____

Q: _____

    A: _____

Q: _____

    A: _____

Account Cheat Sheet

Account	Website	Username	Passcode

©2015 MemoryBanc

Name _____

Security Questions

What is your mother's maiden name? _____

What is your father's first name? _____

What is your grandmother's maiden name? _____

What is your favorite

    food? _____

    movie? _____

    book? _____

What is the name of the town where you were born? _____

What is the name of your first pet? _____

What is the name of your favorite pet? _____

What is the make of your first car? _____

What was your childhood nickname? _____

What is the name of the town where your parents met? _____

What is the name of the city in which you met your spouse or partner?

_____

Use these to document additional security questions (Q) and answers (A):

Q: _____

    A: _____

Q: _____

    A: _____

Q: _____

    A: _____

Q: _____

    A: _____

Account Cheat Sheet

Account	Website	Username	Passcode

©2015 MemoryBanc

Name _____

Email

Account _____ Circle one: Free or Paid

Website _____ PIN _____

Username _____ Passcode _____

Billing information _____

Notes _____

Account _____ Circle one: Free or Paid

Website _____ PIN _____

Username _____ Passcode _____

Billing information _____

Notes _____

Account _____ Circle one: Free or Paid

Website _____ PIN _____

Username _____ Passcode _____

Billing information _____

Notes _____

Account _____ Circle one: Free or Paid

Website _____ PIN _____

Username _____ Passcode _____

Billing information _____

Notes _____

Account _____ Circle one: Free or Paid

Website _____ PIN _____

Username _____ Passcode _____

Billing information _____

Notes _____

Account _____ Circle one: Free or Paid

Website _____ PIN _____

Username _____ Passcode _____

Billing information _____

Notes _____

Account _____ Circle one: Free or Paid

Website _____ PIN _____

Username _____ Passcode _____

Billing information _____

Notes _____

Account _____ Circle one: Free or Paid

Website _____ PIN _____

Username _____ Passcode _____

Billing information _____

Notes _____

Account _____ Circle one: Free or Paid

Website _____ PIN _____

Username _____ Passcode _____

Billing information _____

Notes _____

Account _____ Circle one: Free or Paid

Website _____ PIN _____

Username _____ Passcode _____

Billing information _____

Notes _____

          ©2015 MemoryBanc

Name _____

Email

Account _____ Circle one: Free or Paid

Website _____ PIN _____

Username _____ Passcode _____

Billing information _____

Notes _____

Account _____ Circle one: Free or Paid

Website _____ PIN _____

Username _____ Passcode _____

Billing information _____

Notes _____

Account _____ Circle one: Free or Paid

Website _____ PIN _____

Username _____ Passcode _____

Billing information _____

Notes _____

Account _____ Circle one: Free or Paid

Website _____ PIN _____

Username _____ Passcode _____

Billing information _____

Notes _____

Account _____ Circle one: Free or Paid

Website _____ PIN _____

Username _____ Passcode _____

Billing information _____

Notes _____

Account _____ Circle one: Free or Paid

Website _____ PIN _____

Username _____ Passcode _____

Billing information _____

Notes _____

Account _____ Circle one: Free or Paid

Website _____ PIN _____

Username _____ Passcode _____

Billing information _____

Notes _____

Account _____ Circle one: Free or Paid

Website _____ PIN _____

Username _____ Passcode _____

Billing information _____

Notes _____

Account _____ Circle one: Free or Paid

Website _____ PIN _____

Username _____ Passcode _____

Billing information _____

Notes _____

Account _____ Circle one: Free or Paid

Website _____ PIN _____

Username _____ Passcode _____

Billing information _____

Notes _____

©2015 MemoryBanc

Name _____

Social Media
(Services like Facebook, Twitter & Pinterest)

Account _____ Circle one: Free or Paid

Website _____ PIN _____

Username _____ Passcode _____

Billing information _____

Notes _____

Account _____ Circle one: Free or Paid

Website _____ PIN _____

Username _____ Passcode _____

Billing information _____

Notes _____

Account _____ Circle one: Free or Paid

Website _____ PIN _____

Username _____ Passcode _____

Billing information _____

Notes _____

Account _____ Circle one: Free or Paid

Website _____ PIN _____

Username _____ Passcode _____

Billing information _____

Notes _____

Social Media (cont.)

Account _____ Circle one: Free or Paid

Website _____ PIN _____

Username _____ Passcode _____

Billing information _____

Notes _____

Account _____ Circle one: Free or Paid

Website _____ PIN _____

Username _____ Passcode _____

Billing information _____

Notes _____

Account _____ Circle one: Free or Paid

Website _____ PIN _____

Username _____ Passcode _____

Billing information _____

Notes _____

Account _____ Circle one: Free or Paid

Website _____ PIN _____

Username _____ Passcode _____

Billing information _____

Notes _____

Account _____ Circle one: Free or Paid

Website _____ PIN _____

Username _____ Passcode _____

Billing information _____

©2015 MemoryBanc

Name _____

Social Media
(Services like Facebook, Twitter & Pinterest)

Account _____ Circle one: Free or Paid

Website _____ PIN _____

Username _____ Passcode _____

Billing information _____

Notes _____

Account _____ Circle one: Free or Paid

Website _____ PIN _____

Username _____ Passcode _____

Billing information _____

Notes _____

Account _____ Circle one: Free or Paid

Website _____ PIN _____

Username _____ Passcode _____

Billing information _____

Notes _____

Account _____ Circle one: Free or Paid

Website _____ PIN _____

Username _____ Passcode _____

Billing information _____

Notes _____

Social Media (cont.)

Account _____ Circle one: Free or Paid

Website _____ PIN _____

Username _____ Passcode _____

Billing information _____

Notes _____

Account _____ Circle one: Free or Paid

Website _____ PIN _____

Username _____ Passcode _____

Billing information _____

Notes _____

Account _____ Circle one: Free or Paid

Website _____ PIN _____

Username _____ Passcode _____

Billing information _____

Notes _____

Account _____ Circle one: Free or Paid

Website _____ PIN _____

Username _____ Passcode _____

Billing information _____

Notes _____

Account _____ Circle one: Free or Paid

Website _____ PIN _____

Username _____ Passcode _____

Billing information _____

©2015 MemoryBanc

Name _____

Online Services
(Services like Shutterfly, Amazon & iTunes)

Account _____ Circle one: Free or Paid

Website _____ PIN _____

Username _____ Passcode _____

Billing information _____

Notes _____

Account _____ Circle one: Free or Paid

Website _____ PIN _____

Username _____ Passcode _____

Billing information _____

Notes _____

Account _____ Circle one: Free or Paid

Website _____ PIN _____

Username _____ Passcode _____

Billing information _____

Notes _____

Account _____ Circle one: Free or Paid

Website _____ PIN _____

Username _____ Passcode _____

Billing information _____

Notes _____

Online Services (cont.)

Account _____ Circle one: Free or Paid

Website _____ PIN _____

Username _____ Passcode _____

Billing information _____

Notes _____

Account _____ Circle one: Free or Paid

Website _____ PIN _____

Username _____ Passcode _____

Billing information _____

Notes _____

Account _____ Circle one: Free or Paid

Website _____ PIN _____

Username _____ Passcode _____

Billing information _____

Notes _____

Account _____ Circle one: Free or Paid

Website _____ PIN _____

Username _____ Passcode _____

Billing information _____

Notes _____

©2015 MemoryBanc

Name _____

Online Services
(Services like Shutterfly, Amazon & iTunes)

Account _____ Circle one: Free or Paid

Website _____ PIN _____

Username _____ Passcode _____

Billing information _____

Notes _____

Account _____ Circle one: Free or Paid

Website _____ PIN _____

Username _____ Passcode _____

Billing information _____

Notes _____

Account _____ Circle one: Free or Paid

Website _____ PIN _____

Username _____ Passcode _____

Billing information _____

Notes _____

Account _____ Circle one: Free or Paid

Website _____ PIN _____

Username _____ Passcode _____

Billing information _____

Notes _____

Online Services (cont.)

Account _____ Circle one: Free or Paid

Website _____ PIN _____

Username _____ Passcode _____

Billing information _____

Notes _____

Account _____ Circle one: Free or Paid

Website _____ PIN _____

Username _____ Passcode _____

Billing information _____

Notes _____

Account _____ Circle one: Free or Paid

Website _____ PIN _____

Username _____ Passcode _____

Billing information _____

Notes _____

Account _____ Circle one: Free or Paid

Website _____ PIN _____

Username _____ Passcode _____

Billing information _____

Notes _____

©2015 MemoryBanc

Name _____

Online Services
(Services like Shutterfly, Amazon & iTunes)

Account _____ Circle one: Free or Paid

Website _____ PIN _____

Username _____ Passcode _____

Billing information _____

Notes _____

Account _____ Circle one: Free or Paid

Website _____ PIN _____

Username _____ Passcode _____

Billing information _____

Notes _____

Account _____ Circle one: Free or Paid

Website _____ PIN _____

Username _____ Passcode _____

Billing information _____

Notes _____

Account _____ Circle one: Free or Paid

Website _____ PIN _____

Username _____ Passcode _____

Billing information _____

Notes _____

Online Services (cont.)

Account _____ Circle one: Free or Paid

Website _____ PIN _____

Username _____ Passcode _____

Billing information _____

Notes _____

Account _____ Circle one: Free or Paid

Website _____ PIN _____

Username _____ Passcode _____

Billing information _____

Notes _____

Account _____ Circle one: Free or Paid

Website _____ PIN _____

Username _____ Passcode _____

Billing information _____

Notes _____

Account _____ Circle one: Free or Paid

Website _____ PIN _____

Username _____ Passcode _____

Billing information _____

Notes _____

©2015 MemoryBanc

Name _____

Online Services
(Services like Shutterfly, Amazon & iTunes)

Account _____ Circle one: Free or Paid

Website _____ PIN _____

Username _____ Passcode _____

Billing information _____

Notes _____

Account _____ Circle one: Free or Paid

Website _____ PIN _____

Username _____ Passcode _____

Billing information _____

Notes _____

Account _____ Circle one: Free or Paid

Website _____ PIN _____

Username _____ Passcode _____

Billing information _____

Notes _____

Account _____ Circle one: Free or Paid

Website _____ PIN _____

Username _____ Passcode _____

Billing information _____

Notes _____

Online Services (cont.)

Account _____ Circle one: Free or Paid

Website _____ PIN _____

Username _____ Passcode _____

Billing information _____

Notes _____

Account _____ Circle one: Free or Paid

Website _____ PIN _____

Username _____ Passcode _____

Billing information _____

Notes _____

Account _____ Circle one: Free or Paid

Website _____ PIN _____

Username _____ Passcode _____

Billing information _____

Notes _____

Account _____ Circle one: Free or Paid

Website _____ PIN _____

Username _____ Passcode _____

Billing information _____

Notes _____

©2015 MemoryBanc

Frequently Asked Questions about Online Passcodes and Access

Q: All my passcodes are stored in a passcode app on my phone. Do I still need to document them?

A: Absolutely. Unfortunately, if you are unable to access your passcode keeper, no one will be able to access your accounts. Most "user agreements" preclude others from getting access to your account. The only real way to ensure this information is shared is for you to document it. Some apps allow you to set up access for others as well as print out a cheat sheet. Find out if your app has these features and include a copy with your completed workbook.

Q: I have read that you should never write down your passcodes. Why are you suggesting I document them?

A: Most of the guidance you receive relates to professionals employed within a business. At home, you don't have an IT department that can override and reset your passcodes. I have yet to hear of a thief entering a home and stealing a list of passcodes, but I have heard stories of sorrow over lost pictures and emails as well as frustration over a Facebook or LinkedIn profile that survives past the life of a loved one. For those reasons, I urge you to consider documenting your passcodes.

Remember, I'm not suggesting you walk around with the passcodes in your wallet. The sheet should be kept in a safe place in your home where your loved ones can get to it if necessary.

Q: My estate planning included the designation for a "digital executor," who I understand will provide the legal rights to access my accounts. Is it OK for me to skip this step?

A: Having a "digital executor" is becoming more popular, but most of the online services and account access you have established are governed by the "user terms and agreement" you accepted. If you took the time to read them, you would find that most of the services do not allow you to share access or grant rights to your access to someone else. For this reason, we recommend you write passcodes down.

Q: My passcodes change all the time—how am I supposed to keep up with them?

A: Exactly! This is a major challenge for us all. Once you document your usernames and passcodes, you will find that they really don't change that frequently—unless you are constantly resetting them because you forgot the original passcode. I keep a printout of my list next to my computer, and with more than 80 online accounts and passcodes, I refer to it frequently.

There are several apps that can store your passcodes. I have tried *Password Manager* and *Dashlane*; both require a passcode to access the information so it will only be useful to those who know you use it and who know your login passcode. I recommend you document your most important passcodes in writing because the requirement of a passcode may prove to be a barrier to those you are expecting to step in and assist you. I found having a written list next to my workspace was faster than trying to look up access codes online. I hope you find the solution that works best for you.

CHAPTER 5

Medical Section

Building a Healthcare Profile: Documenting Your Medical History

We're long past living in a world where one general practitioner handles—and keeps track of—all ills, from birth to death. Today, we move throughout our lives and have a variety of healthcare providers working in highly specialized fields. It's really up to you to represent your medical history accurately. And if you have a child or have stepped in to be a medical advocate for a loved one, you know that it's essential to have the key details of an individual's medical history.

The following pages will take you through both a personal medical history as well as a family medical history. Additional forms are available to list doctors and specialists, as well as medications, all of which will prove helpful for general healthcare as well as any more serious medical situations.

The first section, which covers how to use your medical insurance, may be the most crucial. Typically, insurers have online, self-service portals. I recommend that you set these up now—before you need them in an emergency—with documented usernames, passcodes, and PINs. You can easily find lists of providers and specialists, download forms, and even confirm claims.

If you have prescription medications or a medical condition that emergency responders should be aware of, be sure to describe it on your phone under the heading of "ICE" (In Case of Emergency). Many emergency personnel and first responders are trained to look for identifiers about you in your wallet and on your phone, and "ICE" has become a simple way to share this information. If you use a passcode to access your phone, look for downloadable apps that let you set up a screen saver that will display the needed information on the passcode screen for quick access.

Name _____

Health Insurance

HEALTH INSURANCE

Provider name _____ Provider phone (_____) _____

Provider address _____

Policy # _____ Group # _____

Copay _____ Cost/Month $ _____

Website _____ PIN _____

Username _____ Passcode _____

If you are not the primary insured on this account, detail

    Primary insured's name _____ Date of birth _____ / _____ /_____

    Social Security number _____-_____-_____

SUPPLEMENTAL HEALTH INSURANCE

Provider name _____ Provider phone (_____) _____

Provider address _____

Policy # _____ Group # _____

Copay _____ Cost/Month $ _____

Website _____ PIN _____

Username _____ Passcode _____

If you are not the primary insured on this account, detail

    Primary insured's name _____ Date of birth _____ / _____ /_____

    Social Security number _____-_____-_____

_____

_____

_____

_____

_____

DENTAL INSURANCE (if different)

Provider name _____ Provider phone (_____) _____

Provider address _____

Policy # _____ Group # _____

Copay _____ Cost/Month $ _____

Website _____ PIN _____

Username _____ Passcode _____

If you are not the primary insured on this account, detail

    Primary insured's name _____ Date of birth _____ / _____ /_____

    Social Security number _____-_____-_____

VISION INSURANCE (if different)

Provider name _____ Provider phone (_____) _____

Provider address _____

Policy # _____ Group # _____

Copay _____ Cost/Month $ _____

Website _____ PIN _____

Username _____ Passcode _____

If you are not the primary insured on this account, detail

    Primary insured's name _____ Date of birth _____ / _____ /_____

    Social Security number _____-_____-_____

_____

_____

_____

_____

_____

_____

 ©2015 MemoryBanc

Name _____

Health Insurance (cont.)

LONG-TERM CARE INSURANCE

Provider name _____ Provider phone (_____) _____

Provider address _____

Policy # _____ Group # _____

Policy location _____

Copay _____ Cost/Month $ _____

Website _____ PIN _____

Username _____ Passcode _____

If you are not the primary insured on this account, detail

    Primary insured's name _____ Date of birth _____ / _____ / _____

    Social Security number _____-_____-_____

DISABILITY INSURANCE

Provider name _____ Provider phone (_____) _____

Provider address _____

Policy # _____ Group # _____

Policy location _____

Copay _____ Cost/Month $ _____

Website _____ PIN _____

Username _____ Passcode _____

_____

_____

_____

_____

_____

Health Insurance (cont.)

OTHER _____

Account holder (if other than yourself) _____

Provider name _____ Provider phone (_____) _____

Provider address _____

Policy # _____ Group # _____

Policy location _____

Copay _____ Cost/Month $ _____

Website _____ PIN _____

Username _____ Passcode _____

OTHER _____

Account holder (if other than yourself) _____

Provider name _____ Provider phone (_____) _____

Provider address _____

Policy # _____ Group # _____

Policy location _____

Copay _____ Cost/Month $ _____

Website _____ PIN _____

Username _____ Passcode _____

_____

_____

_____

_____

_____

_____

_____

_____

©2015 MemoryBanc

Name _____

Health Insurance

HEALTH INSURANCE

Provider name _____ Provider phone (_____) _____

Provider address _____

Policy # _____ Group # _____

Copay _____ Cost/Month $ _____

Website _____ PIN _____

Username _____ Passcode _____

If you are not the primary insured on this account, detail

    Primary insured's name _____ Date of birth _____ / _____ /_____

    Social Security number _____-_____-_____

SUPPLEMENTAL HEALTH INSURANCE

Provider name _____ Provider phone (_____) _____

Provider address _____

Policy # _____ Group # _____

Copay _____ Cost/Month $ _____

Website _____ PIN _____

Username _____ Passcode _____

If you are not the primary insured on this account, detail

    Primary insured's name _____ Date of birth _____ / _____ /_____

    Social Security number _____-_____-_____

_____
_____
_____
_____
_____

DENTAL INSURANCE (if different)

Provider name _____ Provider phone (_____) _____

Provider address _____

Policy # _____ Group # _____

Copay _____ Cost/Month $ _____

Website _____ PIN _____

Username _____ Passcode _____

If you are not the primary insured on this account, detail

    Primary insured's name _____ Date of birth _____ / _____ /_____

    Social Security number _____-_____-_____

VISION INSURANCE (if different)

Provider name _____ Provider phone (_____) _____

Provider address _____

Policy # _____ Group # _____

Copay _____ Cost/Month $ _____

Website _____ PIN _____

Username _____ Passcode _____

If you are not the primary insured on this account, detail

    Primary insured's name _____ Date of birth _____ / _____ /_____

    Social Security number _____-_____-_____

_____

_____

_____

_____

_____

_____

©2015 MemoryBanc

Name _____

Health Insurance (cont.)

LONG-TERM CARE INSURANCE

Provider name _____ Provider phone (_____) _____

Provider address _____

Policy # _____ Group # _____

Policy location _____

Copay _____ Cost/Month $ _____

Website _____ PIN _____

Username _____ Passcode _____

If you are not the primary insured on this account, detail

    Primary insured's name _____ Date of birth _____ / _____ / _____

    Social Security number _____-_____-_____

DISABILITY INSURANCE

Provider name _____ Provider phone (_____) _____

Provider address _____

Policy # _____ Group # _____

Policy location _____

Copay _____ Cost/Month $ _____

Website _____ PIN _____

Username _____ Passcode _____

_____

_____

_____

_____

_____

Health Insurance (cont.)

OTHER _____

Account holder (if other than yourself) _____

Provider name _____ Provider phone (_____) _____

Provider address _____

Policy # _____ Group # _____

Policy location _____

Copay _____ Cost/Month $ _____

Website _____ PIN _____

Username _____ Passcode _____

OTHER _____

Account holder (if other than yourself) _____

Provider name _____ Provider phone (_____) _____

Provider address _____

Policy # _____ Group # _____

Policy location _____

Copay _____ Cost/Month $ _____

Website _____ PIN _____

Username _____ Passcode _____

_____

_____

_____

_____

_____

_____

_____

_____

©2015 MemoryBanc

Name _____

Healthcare Providers

Details for all doctors, dentists, therapists, and alternative healing contacts

PRIMARY CARE PHYSICIAN

Name/Practice _____ Phone (_____) _____

Address _____

Website _____ Email _____

Hours _____

Notes _____

DENTIST

Name/Practice _____ Phone (_____) _____

Address _____

Website _____ Email _____

Hours _____

Notes _____

OTHER _____

(Specify services provided and root cause for seeing this individual/practice)

Name/Practice _____ Phone (_____) _____

Address _____

Website _____ Email _____

Hours _____

Notes _____

_____

_____

_____

_____

_____

OTHER _____

(Specify services provided and root cause for seeing this individual/practice)

Name/Practice _____ Phone (_____) _____

Address _____

Website _____ Email _____

Hours _____

Notes _____

OTHER _____

(Specify services provided and root cause for seeing this individual/practice)

Name/Practice _____ Phone (_____) _____

Address _____

Website _____ Email _____

Hours _____

Notes _____

OTHER _____

(Specify services provided and root cause for seeing this individual/practice)

Name/Practice _____ Phone (_____) _____

Address _____

Website _____ Email _____

Hours _____

Notes _____

_____

_____

_____

_____

_____

   ©2015 MemoryBanc

Name _____

Healthcare Providers

Details for all doctors, dentists, therapists, and alternative healing contacts

PRIMARY CARE PHYSICIAN

Name/Practice _____ Phone (_____) _____

Address _____

Website _____ Email _____

Hours _____

Notes _____

DENTIST

Name/Practice _____ Phone (_____) _____

Address _____

Website _____ Email _____

Hours _____

Notes _____

OTHER _____

(Specify services provided and root cause for seeing this individual/practice)

Name/Practice _____ Phone (_____) _____

Address _____

Website _____ Email _____

Hours _____

Notes _____

_____

_____

_____

_____

_____

OTHER _____
(Specify services provided and root cause for seeing this individual/practice)

Name/Practice _____ Phone (_____) _____

Address _____

Website _____ Email _____

Hours _____

Notes _____

OTHER _____
(Specify services provided and root cause for seeing this individual/practice)

Name/Practice _____ Phone (_____) _____

Address _____

Website _____ Email _____

Hours _____

Notes _____

OTHER _____
(Specify services provided and root cause for seeing this individual/practice)

Name/Practice _____ Phone (_____) _____

Address _____

Website _____ Email _____

Hours _____

Notes _____

_____

_____

_____

_____

_____

©2015 MemoryBanc

Name _____

Personal Medical History

In order to complete new patient forms, please note the following medical problems and approximate date of illness or diagnosis.

_____ Alcoholism   Diagnosed _____

_____ Cancer; type   Diagnosed _____

_____ Coagulation (bleeding/clotting) disorder   Diagnosed _____

_____ Congenital Heart Disease; type   Diagnosed _____

_____ Diabetes; type _____   Diagnosed _____

_____ Depression/suicide attempt   Date(s) of occurrence(s) _____

_____ High Cholesterol   Diagnosed _____

_____ Hypertension (high blood pressure)   Diagnosed _____

_____ Myocardial Infarction (heart attack)   Date(s) of occurrence(s) _____

_____ Stroke   Date(s) of occurrence(s) _____

_____ Thyroid problem; type   Diagnosed _____

_____ Other _____   Diagnosed _____

_____ Other _____   Diagnosed _____

Additional notes related to the above information _____

Have you ever had a blood transfusion? If so, when? _____

ALLERGIES

Known allergies or reactions to medicines/foods/other	Reaction or side effect

Currently prescribed treatments

Oral Antihistamine _____ EpiPen _____ Other _____

Notes _____

©2015 MemoryBanc

Surgical history	Date

SOCIAL HISTORY

Tobacco Use

Cigarettes   Start date _____ / _____ / _____

                    Quit date _____ / _____ / _____   Packs a day _____

Other Tobacco (pipe/cigar/snuff/chew/other _____)

                    Start date _____ / _____ / _____

                    Quit date _____ / _____ / _____

Alcohol Use   Start date _____ / _____ / _____

                    Quit date _____ / _____ / _____   Drinks/week _____

Exercise   Do you exercise regularly? _____ How often? _____

WOMEN'S GYNECOLOGIC HISTORY

of pregnancies _____   # of deliveries _____   # of miscarriages _____

Age periods began _____ Age periods ended _____

Abnormal Pap smear? Date _____ / _____ / _____

Notes _____

©2015 MemoryBanc

Name _____

Personal Medical History

In order to complete new patient forms, please note the following medical problems and approximate date of illness or diagnosis.

_____ Alcoholism	Diagnosed _____
_____ Cancer; type	Diagnosed _____
_____ Coagulation (bleeding/clotting) disorder	Diagnosed _____
_____ Congenital Heart Disease; type	Diagnosed _____
_____ Diabetes; type _____	Diagnosed _____
_____ Depression/suicide attempt	Date(s) of occurrence(s) _____
_____ High Cholesterol	Diagnosed _____
_____ Hypertension (high blood pressure)	Diagnosed _____
_____ Myocardial Infarction (heart attack)	Date(s) of occurrence(s) _____
_____ Stroke	Date(s) of occurrence(s) _____
_____ Thyroid problem; type	Diagnosed _____
_____ Other _____	Diagnosed _____
_____ Other _____	Diagnosed _____

Additional notes related to the above information _____

Have you ever had a blood transfusion? If so, when? _____

ALLERGIES

Known allergies or reactions to medicines/foods/other	Reaction or side effect

Currently prescribed treatments

Oral Antihistamine _____ EpiPen _____ Other _____

Notes _____

Surgical history	Date

SOCIAL HISTORY

Tobacco Use

Cigarettes   Start date _____ / _____ / _____

                             Quit date _____ / _____ / _____   Packs a day _____

Other Tobacco (pipe/cigar/snuff/chew/other _____)

                             Start date _____ / _____ / _____

                             Quit date _____ / _____ / _____

Alcohol Use   Start date _____ / _____ / _____

                             Quit date _____ / _____ / _____   Drinks/week _____

Exercise   Do you exercise regularly? _____ How often? _____

WOMEN'S GYNECOLOGIC HISTORY

of pregnancies _____   # of deliveries _____   # of miscarriages _____

Age periods began _____ Age periods ended _____

Abnormal Pap smear? Date _____ / _____ / _____

Notes _____

              ©2015 MemoryBanc

Name _____

Current Medications and Supplements

MEDICATIONS

Prescription Include prescribing physician	Treats	Dose	Times per day

VITAMINS, HERBS, AND OTHER SUPPLEMENTS

Name of supplement	Purpose	Dose	Times per day

©2015 MemoryBanc

Name _____

Current Medications and Supplements

MEDICATIONS

Prescription Include prescribing physician	Treats	Dose	Times per day

VITAMINS, HERBS, AND OTHER SUPPLEMENTS

Name of supplement	Purpose	Dose	Times per day

© MemoryBanc 2015

Name _____

Family Medical History

MEDICAL CONDITION	Parent	Sibling	Children	Grandparent	Other
Alcoholism					
Anemia					
Anesthesia problem					
Arthritis					
Asthma					
Birth defects					
Bleeding problem					
Cancer (Breast)					
Cancer (Colon)					
Cancer (Melanoma)					
Cancer (Skin)					
Cancer (Ovary)					
Cancer (Prostate)					
Cancer (unknown)					
Depression					
Diabetes Type 1					
Diabetes Type 2					
Eczema					
Epilepsy/Seizures					
Genetic diseases					
Glaucoma					
Hay Fever/Rhinitis					
Hearing problems					
Heart Attack					
High Blood Pressure					
High Cholesterol					
Kidney disease					

Family Medical History (cont.)

MEDICAL CONDITION	Parent	Sibling	Children	Grandparent	Other
Lupus					
Mental Retardation					
Migraine headaches					
Mitral Valve Prolapse					
Osteoarthritis					
Osteoporosis					
Rheumatoid arthritis					
Stroke					
Thyroid disorder					
Tuberculosis					
Other					
Other					
Other					

Additional notes on any of the listed conditions

_____

_____

_____

_____

Organ Donation? Yes/No

_____

_____

_____

©2015 MemoryBanc

Name _____

Family Medical History

MEDICAL CONDITION	Parent	Sibling	Children	Grandparent	Other
Alcoholism					
Anemia					
Anesthesia problem					
Arthritis					
Asthma					
Birth defects					
Bleeding problem					
Cancer (Breast)					
Cancer (Colon)					
Cancer (Melanoma)					
Cancer (Skin)					
Cancer (Ovary)					
Cancer (Prostate)					
Cancer (unknown)					
Depression					
Diabetes Type 1					
Diabetes Type 2					
Eczema					
Epilepsy/Seizures					
Genetic diseases					
Glaucoma					
Hay Fever/Rhinitis					
Hearing problems					
Heart Attack					
High Blood Pressure					
High Cholesterol					
Kidney disease					

Family Medical History (cont.)

MEDICAL CONDITION	Parent	Sibling	Children	Grandparent	Other
Lupus					
Mental Retardation					
Migraine headaches					
Mitral Valve Prolapse					
Osteoarthritis					
Osteoporosis					
Rheumatoid arthritis					
Stroke					
Thyroid disorder					
Tuberculosis					
Other					
Other					
Other					

Additional notes on any of the listed conditions

_____

_____

_____

_____

Organ Donation? Yes / No

_____

_____

_____

©2015 MemoryBanc

Name_____

Immunizations

Please list the most recent date of the following immunizations or best estimate of year if unknown.

Annual Flu Shot _____ ; _____ ; _____ ; _____ ; _____ ; _____ ;

_____ ; _____ ; _____ ; _____ ; _____ ;

Hepatitis A _____ ; _____ ; _____ ; _____ ; _____ ; _____ ;

Hepatitis B _____ ; _____ ; _____ ; _____ ; _____ ; _____ ;

Measles _____ ; _____ ; _____ ; _____ ; _____ ; _____ ;

MMR _____ ; _____ ; _____ ; _____ ; _____ ; _____ ;

Mumps _____ ; _____ ; _____ ; _____ ; _____ ; _____ ;

Pneumonia _____ ; _____ ; _____ ; _____ ; _____ ; _____ ;

Rubella _____ ; _____ ; _____ ; _____ ; _____ ; _____ ;

Shingles _____ ; _____ ; _____ ; _____ ; _____ ; _____ ;

Tetanus (Td) _____ ; _____ ; _____ ; _____ ; _____ ; _____ ;

Varicella (Chicken Pox) ; _____ ; _____ ; _____ ; _____ ; _____ ;

Other _____ ; _____ ; _____ ; _____ ; _____ ; _____ ;

Other _____ ; _____ ; _____ ; _____ ; _____ ; _____ ;

Other _____ ; _____ ; _____ ; _____ ; _____ ; _____ ;

Other _____ ; _____ ; _____ ; _____ ; _____ ; _____ ;

Other _____ ; _____ ; _____ ; _____ ; _____ ; _____ ;

Notes _____

_____

_____

_____

_____

© MemoryBanc 2015

Name _____

Immunizations

Please list the most recent date of the following immunizations or best estimate of year if unknown.

Annual Flu Shot _____ ; _____ ; _____ ; _____ ; _____ ; _____ ;

_____ ; _____ ; _____ ; _____ ; _____ ; _____ ;

Hepatitis A _____ ; _____ ; _____ ; _____ ; _____ ; _____ ;

Hepatitis B _____ ; _____ ; _____ ; _____ ; _____ ; _____ ;

Measles _____ ; _____ ; _____ ; _____ ; _____ ; _____ ;

MMR _____ ; _____ ; _____ ; _____ ; _____ ; _____ ;

Mumps _____ ; _____ ; _____ ; _____ ; _____ ; _____ ;

Pneumonia _____ ; _____ ; _____ ; _____ ; _____ ; _____ ;

Rubella _____ ; _____ ; _____ ; _____ ; _____ ; _____ ;

Shingles _____ ; _____ ; _____ ; _____ ; _____ ; _____ ;

Tetanus (Td) _____ ; _____ ; _____ ; _____ ; _____ ; _____ ;

Varicella (Chicken Pox) ; _____ ; _____ ; _____ ; _____ ; _____ ;

Other _____ ; _____ ; _____ ; _____ ; _____ ; _____ ;

Other _____ ; _____ ; _____ ; _____ ; _____ ; _____ ;

Other _____ ; _____ ; _____ ; _____ ; _____ ; _____ ;

Other _____ ; _____ ; _____ ; _____ ; _____ ; _____ ;

Other _____ ; _____ ; _____ ; _____ ; _____ ; _____ ;

Notes _____

_____

_____

_____

_____

©2015 MemoryBanc

Name _____

Doctor's Visit

Date of visit _____ / _____ / _____

Doctor visited _____

Scheduled for _____

Form completed by _____

Was the appointment based on a specific complaint or was one reported at the time of the visit?

_____

When did it start? _____ / _____ / _____

What are the symptoms? _____ _____

If you have pain, is it a dull ache or stabbing pain? _____

Have you had this problem before? _____ When? _____

What did you do for it? _____

Have there been any recent changes in your life (stress, medicines, food, exercise, etc.)?

_____

_____

Does anyone else at home or work have these symptoms? _____

How concerned are you about the problem? _____

VITAL SIGNS

Weight _____

Temperature _____

Pulse _____

Blood Pressure _____

DIAGNOSIS

What was the diagnosis? _____

What is the recommended treatment? _____

What might happen next? _____

Does this create any issues or limitations? _____

If additional medication, tests, and treatments were prescribed:

    What's the name of the medicine? _____

    How do I take this? _____

    Why do I need it? _____

    What are the risks? _____

    Are there alternatives? _____

    Is any follow-up testing required? If so, what is it? _____

    How do I prepare for it? _____

    Can I phone in for test results? _____

    What happens if I do nothing? _____

NEXT STEPS

Do I need to return for another visit? _____

Are there any danger signs to watch for? _____

Do I need to report back about my condition? _____

What else do I need to know? _____

Additional Notes _____

_____

_____

_____

_____

_____

_____

_____

©2015 MemoryBanc

Name _____

Doctor's Visit

Date of visit _____ / _____ / _____

Doctor visited _____

Scheduled for _____

Form completed by _____

Was the appointment based on a specific complaint or was one reported at the time of the visit?

_____

When did it start? _____ / _____ / _____

What are the symptoms? _____ _____

If you have pain, is it a dull ache or stabbing pain? _____

Have you had this problem before? _____ When? _____

What did you do for it? _____

Have there been any recent changes in your life (stress, medicines, food, exercise, etc.)?

_____

_____

Does anyone else at home or work have these symptoms? _____

How concerned are you about the problem? _____

VITAL SIGNS

Weight _____

Temperature _____

Pulse _____

Blood Pressure _____

DIAGNOSIS

What was the diagnosis? _____

What is the recommended treatment? _____

Doctor's Visit (cont.)

What might happen next? _____

Does this create any issues or limitations? _____

If additional medication, tests, and treatments were prescribed:

    What's the name of the medicine? _____

    How do I take this? _____

    Why do I need it? _____

    What are the risks? _____

    Are there alternatives? _____

    Is any follow-up testing required? If so, what is it? _____

    How do I prepare for it? _____

    Can I phone in for test results? _____

    What happens if I do nothing? _____

NEXT STEPS

Do I need to return for another visit? _____

Are there any danger signs to watch for? _____

Do I need to report back about my condition? _____

What else do I need to know? _____

Additional Notes _____

_____

_____

_____

_____

_____

_____

©2015 MemoryBanc

Frequently Asked Questions about Medical Information

Q: My doctor keeps my records. Why do I need to document this information too?

A: From past personal experience and also from conversations with many doctors, I have found that the unfortunate reality is that many physicians just don't have the time to review all of your medical details before your visit. Typically, your appointment begins with a physician's assistant, who screens you and takes your vital signs while asking you to recite your medical history and report any issues. In most cases, the assistant follows your lead and may not probe to see whether you have other concerns. Obviously, this conversation can be even trickier if you or a loved one has difficulty speaking or understanding the questions.

As a mother of two children, I deliver most of their medical history and cite their medications. As a caregiver, I needed to be able to recite my parents' medications and medical histories. Having it documented made it easy for me to provide this information and hand it to a sibling who filled in as caregiver when I was away.

Documenting the details makes it easy for you to recall dates, doses, and family history, and it provides important data to anyone who may need to provide this information on your behalf in a crisis.

Q: Why don't you include blood type on your form?

A: Very few medical forms ask for your blood type since any procedure that would involve blood work requires a blood test to confirm type and pathology.

Q: Will I be able to share the documented medical information on behalf of someone else without a healthcare proxy or a power of attorney?

A: Most medical offices will follow the lead of the patient and value the support of loved ones. I was asked only once to provide documentation when visiting medical offices with my parents, and that was when I was asking for a copy of their records. I kept paper versions in my car and had a scanned copy on my phone that I could easily forward when requested. In general, the medical community was very accepting when I was providing medical information for my parents.

However, I have heard families share their difficulties in helping a parent or loved one, and suggest you consult with an estate lawyer to understand how not having these documents could impact you.

CHAPTER 6

Household Section

**Sharing the Keys to the Castle:
Collecting a Household Inventory**

One of the benefits of using this organizing system is the ability to keep track of home repair services and vendors with whom you're satisfied as well as those you would never use again.

In the past year, I saved hundreds of dollars because I was able to get my refrigerator repaired and my dishwasher replaced under warranties that I could easily find.

Storing all of your key household details in one place makes it easy for you and your loved ones who need to follow up on a service call, warranty, or repair. For example, your dishwasher is leaking. It is under warranty and you've called the repair service. Then you unexpectedly have to travel out of town, and when the technician comes to make the repair, a visit fee is charged. If you documented the warranty and other pertinent information (like fees), your family member will be able to easily handle this situation.

You will find several pages dedicated to the collection of everything house related, ranging from the details of home services you might receive, such as cleaning or food delivery, to the details about your vehicles, heating, cooling, garage door, or big-ticket appliances like a range or refrigerator.

You should list any associated account numbers, billing cycle, contact information, and average fees. Some services, like food/grocery delivery, may have an online ordering system and documentation where a username, passcode, and PIN is recommended or required.

You might also want to include these other documents:

- Home and land deeds
- Documentation on any home or land improvements with receipts
- Homeowner association (HOA) documents
- Work orders and contracts on home repairs and improvements

Service Address_____

Home Services

CLEANING SERVICE

Provider name _____

Provider address _____

Provider contact _____ Phone (_____) _____

Account ID _____ Cleaning cycle (weekly/monthly) _____

Notes _____

MEAL SERVICES

Provider name _____

Provider address _____

Provider contact _____ Phone (_____) _____

Account ID _____

Notes _____

PLUMBER

Provider name _____

Provider address _____

Provider contact _____ Phone (_____) _____

Account ID _____

Notes _____

ELECTRICIAN

Provider name _____

Provider address _____

Provider contact _____ Phone (_____) _____

Account ID _____

Notes _____

Home Services (cont.)

OTHER _____

Provider name _____

Provider address _____

Provider contact _____ Phone (_____) _____

Account ID _____

Notes _____

OTHER _____

Provider name _____

Provider address _____

Provider contact _____ Phone (_____) _____

Account ID _____

Notes _____

OTHER _____

Provider name _____

Provider address _____

Provider contact _____ Phone (_____) _____

Account ID _____

Notes _____

OTHER _____

Provider name _____

Provider address _____

Provider contact _____ Phone (_____) _____

Account ID _____

Notes _____

 ©2015 MemoryBanc

Service Address_____

Air Conditioning/Cooling

Item _____ Install date _____

Make/Model _____ Serial number _____

Purchased from _____ Warranty date _____

Please attach copies of your receipts or service plans.

If under warranty or service plan, contact _____

Notes _____

SERVICE TECHNICIANS OR FIRMS

Name _____ Phone(_____) _____

Would you use them again? _____

Notes _____

Name _____ Phone(_____) _____

Would you use them again? _____

Notes _____

Name _____ Phone(_____) _____

Would you use them again? _____

Notes _____

Name _____ Phone(_____) _____

Would you use them again? _____

Notes _____

Name _____ Phone(_____) _____

Would you use them again? _____

Notes _____

Service dates

Service comments

_____ / _____ / _____

_____ / _____ / _____

_____ / _____ / _____

_____ / _____ / _____

_____ / _____ / _____

_____ / _____ / _____

_____ / _____ / _____

_____ / _____ / _____

_____ / _____ / _____

_____ / _____ / _____

©2015 MemoryBanc

Service Address_____

Air Conditioning/Cooling

Item _____ Install date _____

Make/Model _____ Serial number _____

Purchased from _____ Warranty date_____

Please attach copies of your receipts or service plans.

If under warranty or service plan, contact _____

Notes _____

SERVICE TECHNICIANS OR FIRMS

Name _____ Phone(_____) _____

Would you use them again? _____

Notes _____

Name _____ Phone(_____) _____

Would you use them again? _____

Notes _____

Name _____ Phone(_____) _____

Would you use them again? _____

Notes _____

Name _____ Phone(_____) _____

Would you use them again? _____

Notes _____

Name _____ Phone(_____) _____

Would you use them again? _____

Notes _____

Air Conditioning/Cooling (cont.)

Service dates

Service comments

_____ / _____ / _____

_____

_____

_____ / _____ / _____

_____

_____

_____ / _____ / _____

_____

_____

_____ / _____ / _____

_____

_____

_____ / _____ / _____

_____

_____

_____ / _____ / _____

_____

_____

_____ / _____ / _____

_____

_____

_____ / _____ / _____

_____

_____

_____ / _____ / _____

_____

_____

_____ / _____ / _____

_____

_____

©2015 MemoryBanc

Service Address_____

Appliances/Electronics

Item _____ Install date _____

Make/Model _____ Serial number _____

Purchased from _____ Warranty date_____

Please attach copies of your receipts or service plans.

If under warranty or service plan, contact _____

Notes _____

SERVICE TECHNICIANS OR FIRMS

Name _____ Phone(_____) _____

Would you use them again? _____

Notes _____

Name _____ Phone(_____) _____

Would you use them again? _____

Notes _____

Name _____ Phone(_____) _____

Would you use them again? _____

Notes _____

Name _____ Phone(_____) _____

Would you use them again? _____

Notes _____

Name _____ Phone(_____) _____

Would you use them again? _____

Notes _____

Service dates

Service comments

_____ / _____ / _____   _____

_____

_____ / _____ / _____   _____

_____

_____ / _____ / _____   _____

_____

_____ / _____ / _____   _____

_____

_____ / _____ / _____   _____

_____

_____ / _____ / _____   _____

_____

_____ / _____ / _____   _____

_____

_____ / _____ / _____   _____

_____

_____ / _____ / _____   _____

_____

_____ / _____ / _____   _____

_____

©2015 MemoryBanc

Service Address_____

Appliances/Electronics

Item _____ Install date _____

Make/Model _____ Serial number _____

Purchased from _____ Warranty date_____

Please attach copies of your receipts or service plans.

If under warranty or service plan, contact _____

Notes _____

SERVICE TECHNICIANS OR FIRMS

Name _____ Phone(_____) _____

Would you use them again? _____

Notes _____

Name _____ Phone(_____) _____

Would you use them again? _____

Notes _____

Name _____ Phone(_____) _____

Would you use them again? _____

Notes _____

Name _____ Phone(_____) _____

Would you use them again? _____

Notes _____

Name _____ Phone(_____) _____

Would you use them again? _____

Notes _____

Appliances/Electronics (cont.)

Service dates   Service comments

_____ / _____ / _____   _____

_____

_____ / _____ / _____   _____

_____

_____ / _____ / _____   _____

_____

_____ / _____ / _____   _____

_____

_____ / _____ / _____   _____

_____

_____ / _____ / _____   _____

_____

_____ / _____ / _____   _____

_____

_____ / _____ / _____   _____

_____

_____ / _____ / _____   _____

_____

_____ / _____ / _____   _____

_____

©2015 MemoryBanc

Service Address_____

Appliances/Electronics

Item _____ Install date _____

Make/Model _____ Serial number _____

Purchased from _____ Warranty date _____

Please attach copies of your receipts or service plans.

If under warranty or service plan, contact _____

Notes _____

SERVICE TECHNICIANS OR FIRMS

Name _____ Phone(_____) _____

Would you use them again? _____

Notes _____

Name _____ Phone(_____) _____

Would you use them again? _____

Notes _____

Name _____ Phone(_____) _____

Would you use them again? _____

Notes _____

Name _____ Phone(_____) _____

Would you use them again? _____

Notes _____

Name _____ Phone(_____) _____

Would you use them again? _____

Notes _____

Service dates

Service comments

_____ / _____ / _____

_____

_____

_____ / _____ / _____

_____

_____

_____ / _____ / _____

_____

_____

_____ / _____ / _____

_____

_____

_____ / _____ / _____

_____

_____

_____ / _____ / _____

_____

_____

_____ / _____ / _____

_____

_____

_____ / _____ / _____

_____

_____

_____ / _____ / _____

_____

_____

_____ / _____ / _____

_____

_____

©2015 MemoryBanc

Service Address_____

Appliances/Electronics

Item _____ Install date _____

Make/Model _____ Serial number _____

Purchased from _____ Warranty date_____

Please attach copies of your receipts or service plans.

If under warranty or service plan, contact _____

Notes _____

SERVICE TECHNICIANS OR FIRMS

Name _____ Phone (_____) _____

Would you use them again? _____

Notes _____

Name _____ Phone (_____) _____

Would you use them again? _____

Notes _____

Name _____ Phone (_____) _____

Would you use them again? _____

Notes _____

Name _____ Phone (_____) _____

Would you use them again? _____

Notes _____

Name _____ Phone (_____) _____

Would you use them again? _____

Notes _____

Appliances/Electronics (cont.)

Service dates

Service comments

_____ / _____ / _____

_____ / _____ / _____

_____ / _____ / _____

_____ / _____ / _____

_____ / _____ / _____

_____ / _____ / _____

_____ / _____ / _____

_____ / _____ / _____

_____ / _____ / _____

_____ / _____ / _____

©2015 MemoryBanc

Service Address_____

Garage Door

Item _____ Install date _____

Make/Model _____ Serial number _____

Purchased from _____ Warranty date_____

Please attach copies of your receipts or service plans.

If under warranty or service plan, contact _____

Notes _____

SERVICE TECHNICIANS OR FIRMS

Name _____ Phone(_____) _____

Would you use them again? _____

Notes _____

Name _____ Phone(_____) _____

Would you use them again? _____

Notes _____

Name _____ Phone(_____) _____

Would you use them again? _____

Notes _____

Name _____ Phone(_____) _____

Would you use them again? _____

Notes _____

Name _____ Phone(_____) _____

Would you use them again? _____

Notes _____

Service dates   Service comments

_____ / _____ / _____   _____

_____

_____ / _____ / _____   _____

_____

_____ / _____ / _____   _____

_____

_____ / _____ / _____   _____

_____

_____ / _____ / _____   _____

_____

_____ / _____ / _____   _____

_____

_____ / _____ / _____   _____

_____

_____ / _____ / _____   _____

_____

_____ / _____ / _____   _____

_____

_____ / _____ / _____   _____

_____

     ©2015 MemoryBanc

Service Address_____

Garage Door

Item _____ Install date _____

Make/Model _____ Serial number _____

Purchased from _____ Warranty date_____

Please attach copies of your receipts or service plans.

If under warranty or service plan, contact _____

Notes _____

SERVICE TECHNICIANS OR FIRMS

Name _____ Phone(_____) _____

Would you use them again? _____

Notes _____

Name _____ Phone(_____) _____

Would you use them again? _____

Notes _____

Name _____ Phone(_____) _____

Would you use them again? _____

Notes _____

Name _____ Phone(_____) _____

Would you use them again? _____

Notes _____

Name _____ Phone(_____) _____

Would you use them again? _____

Notes _____

Garage Door (cont.)

Service dates   Service comments

_____ / _____ / _____   _____

_____

_____ / _____ / _____   _____

_____

_____ / _____ / _____   _____

_____

_____ / _____ / _____   _____

_____

_____ / _____ / _____   _____

_____

_____ / _____ / _____   _____

_____

_____ / _____ / _____   _____

_____

_____ / _____ / _____   _____

_____

_____ / _____ / _____   _____

_____

_____ / _____ / _____   _____

_____

                    ©2015 MemoryBanc

Service Address_____

Heat Pump/Furnace

Item _____   Install date _____

Make/Model _____   Serial number _____

Purchased from _____   Warranty date _____

Please attach copies of your receipts or service plans.

If under warranty or service plan, contact _____

Notes _____

SERVICE TECHNICIANS OR FIRMS

Name _____   Phone (_____) _____

Would you use them again? _____

Notes _____

Name _____   Phone (_____) _____

Would you use them again? _____

Notes _____

Name _____   Phone (_____) _____

Would you use them again? _____

Notes _____

Name _____   Phone (_____) _____

Would you use them again? _____

Notes _____

Name _____   Phone (_____) _____

Would you use them again? _____

Notes _____

Service dates   Service comments

_____ / _____ / _____   _____

_____

_____ / _____ / _____   _____

_____

_____ / _____ / _____   _____

_____

_____ / _____ / _____   _____

_____

_____ / _____ / _____   _____

_____

_____ / _____ / _____   _____

_____

_____ / _____ / _____   _____

_____

_____ / _____ / _____   _____

_____

_____ / _____ / _____   _____

_____

_____ / _____ / _____   _____

_____

©2015 MemoryBanc

Service Address_____

Heat Pump/Furnace

Item _____ Install date _____

Make/Model _____ Serial number _____

Purchased from _____ Warranty date_____

Please attach copies of your receipts or service plans.

If under warranty or service plan, contact _____

Notes _____

SERVICE TECHNICIANS OR FIRMS

Name _____ Phone(_____) _____

Would you use them again? _____

Notes _____

Name _____ Phone(_____) _____

Would you use them again? _____

Notes _____

Name _____ Phone(_____) _____

Would you use them again? _____

Notes _____

Name _____ Phone(_____) _____

Would you use them again? _____

Notes _____

Name _____ Phone(_____) _____

Would you use them again? _____

Notes _____

Service dates

Service comments

_____ / _____ / _____

_____ / _____ / _____

_____ / _____ / _____

_____ / _____ / _____

_____ / _____ / _____

_____ / _____ / _____

_____ / _____ / _____

_____ / _____ / _____

_____ / _____ / _____

_____ / _____ / _____

©2015 MemoryBanc

Name _____

Vehicle

This covers vehicle service records. Loan and insurance details are located in the Financial Section.

Year/Make/Model _____ Location _____

Vehicle Identification Number (VIN) _____

License plate number _____ License renewal date _____ , _____ , _____ ,

_____ , _____ , _____ , _____ , _____ , _____ , _____ , _____ , _____ , _____

Inspection renewal date _____ , _____ , _____ , _____ , _____ , _____ , _____ , _____ ,

_____ , _____, _____ , _____ , _____ , _____ , _____ , _____ , _____ , _____

Purchased date _____ Warranty date _____

Location of title documents _____

Warranty details _____

Please add copies of your receipts or service plans.

If under warranty or service plan, contact _____

Notes _____

SERVICE TECHNICIANS OR FIRMS

Name _____ Phone (_____) _____

Would you use them again? _____

Notes _____

Name _____ Phone (_____) _____

Would you use them again? _____

Notes _____

Name _____ Phone (_____) _____

Would you use them again? _____

Notes _____

Vehicle (cont.)

Service dates

Service comments

_____ / _____ / _____   _____

_____

_____ / _____ / _____   _____

_____

_____ / _____ / _____   _____

_____

_____ / _____ / _____   _____

_____

_____ / _____ / _____   _____

_____

_____ / _____ / _____   _____

_____

_____ / _____ / _____   _____

_____

_____ / _____ / _____   _____

_____

_____ / _____ / _____   _____

_____

©2015 MemoryBanc

Name _____

Vehicle

This covers vehicle service records. Loan and insurance details are located in the Financial Section.

Year/Make/Model _____ Location _____

Vehicle Identification Number (VIN) _____

License plate number _____ License renewal date _____ , _____ , _____ ,

_____ , _____ , _____ , _____ , _____ , _____ , _____ , _____ , _____ , _____

Inspection renewal date _____ , _____ , _____ , _____ , _____ , _____ , _____ , _____ ,

_____ , _____, _____ , _____ , _____ , _____ , _____ , _____ , _____ , _____

Purchased date _____ Warranty date _____

Location of title documents _____

Warranty details _____

Please add copies of your receipts or service plans.

If under warranty or service plan, contact _____

Notes _____

SERVICE TECHNICIANS OR FIRMS

Name _____ Phone (_____) _____

Would you use them again? _____

Notes _____

Name _____ Phone (_____) _____

Would you use them again? _____

Notes _____

Name _____ Phone (_____) _____

Would you use them again? _____

Notes _____

Service dates   Service comments

_____ / _____/ _____   _____

_____

_____ / _____/ _____   _____

_____

_____ / _____/ _____   _____

_____

_____ / _____/ _____   _____

_____

_____ / _____/ _____   _____

_____

_____ / _____/ _____   _____

_____

_____ / _____/ _____   _____

_____

_____ / _____/ _____   _____

_____

_____ / _____/ _____   _____

_____

_____ / _____/ _____   _____

_____

©2015 MemoryBanc

Name _____

Vehicle

This covers vehicle service records. Loan and insurance details are located in the Financial Section.

Year/Make/Model _____ Location _____

Vehicle Identification Number (VIN) _____

License plate number _____ License renewal date _____ , _____ , _____ ,

_____ , _____ , _____ , _____ , _____ , _____ , _____ , _____ , _____ , _____

Inspection renewal date _____ , _____ , _____ , _____ , _____ , _____ , _____ , _____ ,

_____ , _____, _____ , _____ , _____ , _____ , _____ , _____ , _____ , _____

Purchased date _____ Warranty date _____

Location of title documents _____

Warranty details _____

Please add copies of your receipts or service plans.

If under warranty or service plan, contact _____

Notes _____

SERVICE TECHNICIANS OR FIRMS

Name _____ Phone (_____) _____

Would you use them again? _____

Notes _____

Name _____ Phone (_____) _____

Would you use them again? _____

Notes _____

Name _____ Phone (_____) _____

Would you use them again? _____

Notes _____

Service dates

Service comments

_____ / _____ / _____   _____

_____

_____ / _____ / _____   _____

_____

_____ / _____ / _____   _____

_____

_____ / _____ / _____   _____

_____

_____ / _____ / _____   _____

_____

_____ / _____ / _____   _____

_____

_____ / _____ / _____   _____

_____

_____ / _____ / _____   _____

_____

_____ / _____ / _____   _____

_____

_____ / _____ / _____   _____

_____

©2015 MemoryBanc

Service Address_____

Other _____

Item _____ Install date _____

Make/Model _____ Serial number _____

Purchased from _____ Warranty date _____

Please attach copies of your receipts or service plans.

If under warranty or service plan, contact _____

Notes _____

SERVICE TECHNICIANS OR FIRMS

Name _____ Phone (_____) _____

Would you use them again? _____

Notes _____

Name _____ Phone (_____) _____

Would you use them again? _____

Notes _____

Name _____ Phone (_____) _____

Would you use them again? _____

Notes _____

Name _____ Phone (_____) _____

Would you use them again? _____

Notes _____

Name _____ Phone (_____) _____

Would you use them again? _____

Notes _____

Other _____ (cont.)

Service dates

Service comments

_____ / _____ / _____

_____ / _____ / _____

_____ / _____ / _____

_____ / _____ / _____

_____ / _____ / _____

_____ / _____ / _____

_____ / _____ / _____

_____ / _____ / _____

_____ / _____ / _____

_____ / _____ / _____

©2015 MemoryBanc

Service Address_____

Other _____

Item _____ Install date _____

Make/Model _____ Serial number _____

Purchased from _____ Warranty date _____

Please attach copies of your receipts or service plans.

If under warranty or service plan, contact _____

Notes _____

SERVICE TECHNICIANS OR FIRMS

Name _____ Phone(_____) _____

Would you use them again? _____

Notes _____

Name _____ Phone(_____) _____

Would you use them again? _____

Notes _____

Name _____ Phone(_____) _____

Would you use them again? _____

Notes _____

Name _____ Phone(_____) _____

Would you use them again? _____

Notes _____

Name _____ Phone(_____) _____

Would you use them again? _____

Notes _____

Other _____ (cont.)

Service dates

_____ / _____ / _____

_____ / _____ / _____

_____ / _____ / _____

_____ / _____ / _____

_____ / _____ / _____

_____ / _____ / _____

_____ / _____ / _____

_____ / _____ / _____

_____ / _____ / _____

_____ / _____ / _____

Service comments

©2015 MemoryBanc

Service Address_____

Other _____

Item _____ Install date _____

Make/Model _____ Serial number _____

Purchased from _____ Warranty date _____

Please attach copies of your receipts or service plans.

If under warranty or service plan, contact _____

Notes _____

SERVICE TECHNICIANS OR FIRMS

Name _____ Phone(_____) _____

Would you use them again? _____

Notes _____

Name _____ Phone(_____) _____

Would you use them again? _____

Notes _____

Name _____ Phone(_____) _____

Would you use them again? _____

Notes _____

Name _____ Phone(_____) _____

Would you use them again? _____

Notes _____

Name _____ Phone(_____) _____

Would you use them again? _____

Notes _____

Other _____ (cont.)

Service dates	Service comments
_____ / _____ / _____	_____
_____ / _____ / _____	_____
_____ / _____ / _____	_____
_____ / _____ / _____	_____
_____ / _____ / _____	_____
_____ / _____ / _____	_____
_____ / _____ / _____	_____
_____ / _____ / _____	_____
_____ / _____ / _____	_____
_____ / _____ / _____	_____

©2015 MemoryBanc

Service Address_____

Other _____

Item _____ Install date _____

Make/Model _____ Serial number _____

Purchased from _____ Warranty date _____

Please attach copies of your receipts or service plans.

If under warranty or service plan, contact _____

Notes _____

SERVICE TECHNICIANS OR FIRMS

Name _____ Phone (_____) _____

Would you use them again? _____

Notes _____

Name _____ Phone (_____) _____

Would you use them again? _____

Notes _____

Name _____ Phone (_____) _____

Would you use them again? _____

Notes _____

Name _____ Phone (_____) _____

Would you use them again? _____

Notes _____

Name _____ Phone (_____) _____

Would you use them again? _____

Notes _____

Other _____ (cont.)

Service dates	Service comments
_____ / _____ / _____	_____
	_____
_____ / _____ / _____	_____
	_____
_____ / _____ / _____	_____
	_____
_____ / _____ / _____	_____
	_____
_____ / _____ / _____	_____
	_____
_____ / _____ / _____	_____
	_____
_____ / _____ / _____	_____
	_____
_____ / _____ / _____	_____
	_____
_____ / _____ / _____	_____
	_____
_____ / _____ / _____	_____
	_____

©2015 MemoryBanc

Frequently Asked Questions about Household Details

Q: We own a home warranty that covers most of the appliances in our home. Where should I record that information?

A: In the Household Section, you will find a directory of services. Use the "Other" listing to include this information. We recommend you list the provider and the contact information in this section and note the home warranty contact information on the Appliance(s) page(s) it covers.

Q: We own more than one property. How should I handle that?

A: You will find each form includes a "Service Address" so that you can document the details related to different properties that you may own or manage.

Q: We have a pool, and I don't see a page listed for that.

A: You will find pages marked "Other" that you can tailor to unique needs as well as use the blank lined sheets to cover additional assets in your household that you manage.

CHAPTER 7

Etcetera

Managing Everything Else:
Covering Memberships to Pet Care Wishes

This section includes the other information that is helpful to have organized in one location. This is a catchall section for miscellaneous items, including important dates, subscriptions, memberships, frequent flyer accounts, personal contacts, weekly schedules, and pet care needs. Whatever details are part of your routine should be incorporated in this section. These are all useful tools in organizing a household.

Several frequent flyer programs can be transferred and could prove to be a valuable asset. Make sure to document those programs to ensure you (or your loved ones) benefit from your loyalty.

For any items you think would be helpful, but are not already included in this workbook, mail your suggestions with any examples to: MemoryBanc, 4601 N. Fairfax Drive, #1200, Arlington, VA 22203.

Name_____

Birthdays and Anniversaries

JANUARY

_____   _____
_____   _____
_____   _____
_____   _____
_____   _____
_____   _____
_____   _____

FEBRUARY

_____   _____
_____   _____
_____   _____
_____   _____
_____   _____
_____   _____
_____   _____

MARCH

_____   _____
_____   _____
_____   _____
_____   _____
_____   _____
_____   _____
_____   _____

APRIL

_____   _____
_____   _____
_____   _____
_____   _____
_____   _____
_____   _____

MAY

_____   _____
_____   _____
_____   _____
_____   _____
_____   _____
_____   _____

JUNE

_____   _____
_____   _____
_____   _____
_____   _____
_____   _____
_____   _____

©2015 MemoryBanc

Birthdays and Anniversaries (cont.)

JULY

_____   _____
_____   _____
_____   _____
_____   _____
_____   _____
_____   _____

AUGUST

_____   _____
_____   _____
_____   _____
_____   _____
_____   _____
_____   _____

SEPTEMBER

_____   _____
_____   _____
_____   _____
_____   _____
_____   _____
_____   _____

OCTOBER

_____   _____
_____   _____
_____   _____
_____   _____
_____   _____
_____   _____
_____   _____

NOVEMBER

_____   _____
_____   _____
_____   _____
_____   _____
_____   _____
_____   _____
_____   _____

DECEMBER

_____   _____
_____   _____
_____   _____
_____   _____
_____   _____
_____   _____
_____   _____

©2015 MemoryBanc

Name _____

Contacts

Name _____

Address _____

Home (_____) _____ Cell (_____) _____

Office (_____) _____ Email _____

Notes _____

Name _____

Address _____

Home (_____) _____ Cell (_____) _____

Office (_____) _____ Email _____

Notes _____

Name _____

Address _____

Home (_____) _____ Cell (_____) _____

Office (_____) _____ Email _____

Notes _____

Name _____

Address _____

Home (_____) _____ Cell (_____) _____

Office (_____) _____ Email _____

Notes _____

Name _____

Address _____

Home (_____) _____ Cell (_____) _____

Office (_____) _____ Email _____

Notes _____

Name _____

Address _____

Home (_____) _____ Cell (_____) _____

Office (_____) _____ Email _____

Notes _____

Name _____

Address _____

Home (_____) _____ Cell (_____) _____

Office (_____) _____ Email _____

Notes _____

Name _____

Address _____

Home (_____) _____ Cell (_____) _____

Office (_____) _____ Email _____

Notes _____

Name _____

Address _____

Home (_____) _____ Cell (_____) _____

Office (_____) _____ Email _____

Notes _____

Name _____

Address _____

Home (_____) _____ Cell (_____) _____

Office (_____) _____ Email _____

Notes _____

©2015 MemoryBanc

Name _____

Contacts

Name _____

Address _____

Home (_____) _____ Cell (_____) _____

Office (_____) _____ Email _____

Notes _____

Name _____

Address _____

Home (_____) _____ Cell (_____) _____

Office (_____) _____ Email _____

Notes _____

Name _____

Address _____

Home (_____) _____ Cell (_____) _____

Office (_____) _____ Email _____

Notes _____

Name _____

Address _____

Home (_____) _____ Cell (_____) _____

Office (_____) _____ Email _____

Notes _____

Name _____

Address _____

Home (_____) _____ Cell (_____) _____

Office (_____) _____ Email _____

Notes _____

Name _____

Address _____

Home (_____) _____ Cell (_____) _____

Office (_____) _____ Email _____

Notes _____

Name _____

Address _____

Home (_____) _____ Cell (_____) _____

Office (_____) _____ Email _____

Notes _____

Name _____

Address _____

Home (_____) _____ Cell (_____) _____

Office (_____) _____ Email _____

Notes _____

Name _____

Address _____

Home (_____) _____ Cell (_____) _____

Office (_____) _____ Email _____

Notes _____

Name _____

Address _____

Home (_____) _____ Cell (_____) _____

Office (_____) _____ Email _____

Notes _____

 ©2015 MemoryBanc

Name _____

Contacts

Name _____

Address _____

Home (_____) _____ Cell (_____) _____

Office (_____) _____ Email _____

Notes _____

Name _____

Address _____

Home (_____) _____ Cell (_____) _____

Office (_____) _____ Email _____

Notes _____

Name _____

Address _____

Home (_____) _____ Cell (_____) _____

Office (_____) _____ Email _____

Notes _____

Name _____

Address _____

Home (_____) _____ Cell (_____) _____

Office (_____) _____ Email _____

Notes _____

Name _____

Address _____

Home (_____) _____ Cell (_____) _____

Office (_____) _____ Email _____

Notes _____

Name _____

Address _____

Home (_____) _____ Cell (_____) _____

Office (_____) _____ Email _____

Notes _____

Name _____

Address _____

Home (_____) _____ Cell (_____) _____

Office (_____) _____ Email _____

Notes _____

Name _____

Address _____

Home (_____) _____ Cell (_____) _____

Office (_____) _____ Email _____

Notes _____

Name _____

Address _____

Home (_____) _____ Cell (_____) _____

Office (_____) _____ Email _____

Notes _____

Name _____

Address _____

Home (_____) _____ Cell (_____) _____

Office (_____) _____ Email _____

Notes _____

 ©2015 MemoryBanc

Name _____

Contacts

Name _____

Address _____

Home (_____) _____ Cell (_____) _____

Office (_____) _____ Email _____

Notes _____

Name _____

Address _____

Home (_____) _____ Cell (_____) _____

Office (_____) _____ Email _____

Notes _____

Name _____

Address _____

Home (_____) _____ Cell (_____) _____

Office (_____) _____ Email _____

Notes _____

Name _____

Address _____

Home (_____) _____ Cell (_____) _____

Office (_____) _____ Email _____

Notes _____

Name _____

Address _____

Home (_____) _____ Cell (_____) _____

Office (_____) _____ Email _____

Notes _____

Name _____

Address _____

Home (_____) _____ Cell (_____) _____

Office (_____) _____ Email _____

Notes _____

Name _____

Address _____

Home (_____) _____ Cell (_____) _____

Office (_____) _____ Email _____

Notes _____

Name _____

Address _____

Home (_____) _____ Cell (_____) _____

Office (_____) _____ Email _____

Notes _____

Name _____

Address _____

Home (_____) _____ Cell (_____) _____

Office (_____) _____ Email _____

Notes _____

Name _____

Address _____

Home (_____) _____ Cell (_____) _____

Office (_____) _____ Email _____

Notes _____

 ©2015 MemoryBanc

Name_____

Frequent Flyer, Hotel and Rental Car Accounts

Account name	Membership number	Estimated points	Contact number and account details

_____
_____
_____
_____
_____
_____
_____
_____
_____
_____
_____

© MemoryBanc 2015

Name _____

Schedule

DAY	AM	PM
Sunday		
Monday		
Tuesday		
Wednesday		
Thursday		
Friday		
Saturday		

©2015 MemoryBanc

Name _____

Subscriptions and Memberships

MAGAZINES/NEWSPAPERS/NEWSLETTERS

Publication name	Renewal date	Contact number or account details

CLUB/GROUPS/SOCIETY MEMBERSHIPS

Organization name	Renewal date	Member number or account details

Additional related details or important information regarding these accounts _____

_____

_____

_____

©2015 MemoryBanc

Pet Name _____

Pet Care

Type of Pet _____ Sex: Male/Female

Breed _____ Color or markings _____

Birth date/Age _____ Weight _____

Neutered? Y/N   Spayed? Y/N   Date_____

VETERINARIAN

Clinic/Name _____ Phone (_____) _____

Address _____

Email _____ Hours _____

Notes _____

PET FOOD/HABITS

Preferred brand _____

Morning quantity _____ Evening quantity _____

Meal habits _____

Known food allergies _____

TEMPORARY/PERMANENT GUARDIANSHIP

In the event I become incapacitated or am disabled and unable to manage my own affairs, I have named this person (other than a spouse) to act as guardian for this pet:

Name _____ Phone (_____) _____

Email _____

Address _____

MEDICAL CONDITIONS

Does your pet have any physical limitations? _____

Does your pet have any chronic medical conditions? _____

Do you do monthly __ Flea/tick prevention __ Heartworm __ Other _____

Medication	Dose	Purpose	Administration method	Refill orders	Times per day

Surgical history	Date

PET BEHAVIOR

Is your pet crate trained? _____

Does your pet socialize with other pets? Y/N Where? _____

How does your pet interact with other pets in the household? _____

How does your pet respond when meeting another pet? _____

Does your pet show aggressive behavior on the leash? _____

How does your pet respond to strangers? _____

Has your pet ever bitten a person or another animal? _____

Is there any behavior a new guardian should be aware of? _____

Please provide any special information or instructions that would be helpful to someone caring for your pet that has not been covered already.

_____

_____

_____

_____

    ©2015 MemoryBanc

Pet Name _____

Pet Care

Type of Pet _____ Sex: Male/Female

Breed _____ Color or markings _____

Birth date/Age _____ Weight _____

Neutered? Y/N   Spayed? Y/N   Date_____

VETERINARIAN

Clinic/Name _____ Phone (_____) _____

Address _____

Email _____ Hours _____

Notes _____

PET FOOD/HABITS

Preferred brand _____

Morning quantity _____ Evening quantity _____

Meal habits _____

Known food allergies _____

TEMPORARY/PERMANENT GUARDIANSHIP

In the event I become incapacitated or am disabled and unable to manage my own affairs, I have named this person (other than a spouse) to act as guardian for this pet:

Name _____ Phone (_____) _____

Email _____

Address _____

MEDICAL CONDITIONS

Does your pet have any physical limitations? _____

Does your pet have any chronic medical conditions? _____

Do you do monthly __ Flea/tick prevention __ Heartworm __ Other _____

Medication	Dose	Purpose	Administration method	Refill orders	Times per day

Surgical history	Date

PET BEHAVIOR

Is your pet crate trained? _____

Does your pet socialize with other pets? Y/N Where? _____

How does your pet interact with other pets in the household? _____

How does your pet respond when meeting another pet? _____

Does your pet show aggressive behavior on the leash? _____

How does your pet respond to strangers? _____

Has your pet ever bitten a person or another animal? _____

Is there any behavior a new guardian should be aware of? _____

Please provide any special information or instructions that would be helpful to someone caring for your pet that has not been covered already.

_____

_____

_____

_____

©2015 MemoryBanc

Frequently Asked Questions about Everything Else

Q: How do others use the Schedule page to track daily activities?

A: The Schedule page was designed to offer you one place to record typical weekly schedules. There are many ways to use the Schedule page. Some owners use it to record service dates, like grocery delivery or cleaning services, and others have used it to clarify activities and interests for children with special needs. I used it for my parents, initially to document their weekly activities, so I could keep track of them and then later to help remind my parents of their scheduled weekly activities.

Q: What is different about "Contacts" versus "Key Contacts" from the Personal Section?

A: The Contacts pages are intended to help you include important loved ones, like relatives and friends, who are part of your everyday life. The "Key Contacts" are those who play specific roles, such as accountants or clergy.

Q: I had an idea for a worksheet that would help others. Do you accept suggestions?

A: Absolutely. The genesis for this workbook initially came from my experience supporting my parents. Since that first version, hundreds of clients, along with estate lawyers and financial planners, have reviewed and made suggestions for additional worksheets. Mail your suggestions with any examples to: MemoryBanc, 4601 N. Fairfax Drive, #1200, Arlington, VA 22203.

©2015 MemoryBanc

©2015 MemoryBanc

©2015 MemoryBanc

©2015 MemoryBanc

©2015 MemoryBanc

APPENDIX

The Basics of Estate Planning

Estate Planning Documents and Their Value

Author's Note: Since I'm not an attorney, I have asked Lori K. Murphy, Esq., to provide an overview of what documents are involved in estate planning and how you can ensure that your wishes with regard to your estate are properly carried out.

Most people know they should have a will so their estate (assets) can be administered and distributed to beneficiaries of their choice after death.

Unfortunately, many people fail to plan for a medical crisis or permanent disability in which they are unable to legally handle their business, financial, and personal affairs. If you do nothing else, you should have a durable power of attorney (DPOA).

The DPOA allows you to choose who will be in control of your affairs, should you be unable to act on your own behalf, as well as assist you should you need support. For example, if someone has a stroke and has difficulty speaking, the person designated in the DPOA would be able to deal with banks and other financial institutions on behalf of the ailing individual. It also helps avoid a court-ordered guardianship or conservatorship for those individuals who need support but don't have a designated agent.

Every person over the age of 18 should have in place an advance directive/healthcare power of attorney. This document spells out what you want done in the event that you are severely ill or injured; it designates someone to make medical decisions should you become incapacitated. This is the document in which you would say whether you want to be kept on life support or "have the plug pulled." Many families learn of this need when their child is away at college. Without it, parents who are providing the medical insurance and paying the bills will find that, because of the Health Insurance Portability and Accountability Act (HIPAA) regulations governing medical personnel, they will be unable to get information on a child's medical needs if they are not with their child.

A disability and even a temporary incapacity can arise from a number of different causes such as illness, injury, an accident, or old age. If this happens—and you have not executed powers of attorney—then the court may decide who will act on your behalf. This is typically a very lengthy and expensive process.

A qualified lawyer can draft these documents tailored specifically to your needs and your state for just a few hundred dollars.

The Importance of Having a Will

Most believe that estate planning is only for wealthy people. However, that is a misconception since a will spells out the division of assets among family members, regardless of the size of the estate. The tools used in estate planning legally protect and distribute property based on your wishes and the needs of your family and/or survivors while minimizing tax consequences. It is also the only legal way that you can establish guardians for your minor children while you are still alive.

Completing a will is the most practical first step in estate planning; it makes clear how you want your property to be distributed after you die. Writing one can be as simple as typing out how you want your assets to be transferred to loved ones or charitable organizations after your death, but be sure to follow your state's formalities. If you don't have a will when you die, your estate will be handled in probate, and your property could be distributed differently than what you would like.

Some states have community property laws that entitle your surviving spouse to keep half of your wealth after you die no matter what percentage you have specified. Because of varying state laws like community property and to avoid any issues in settling your estate, you should consider getting the help of a lawyer who is dedicated to the legal practice of estate planning. Fees for the execution of a will vary according to its complexity.

What Is a Trust?

A trust offers the ability to avoid probate and keep your affairs private. It is a more complex legal vehicle that offers before-death and after-death advantages, as well as providing more control over your assets and their management. It is often an ideal document in which to provide financial support for family members, particularly for second marriages, as well. To find out if a trust is right for your situation, you should consult an attorney.

About Lori K. Murphy

Lori is an attorney licensed in Oregon, Washington, Virginia, and the District of Columbia, and focuses her practice on estate planning and estate administration.

About the Author

Kay Bransford is a recognized expert in how to collect, manage, and organize personal information. *Forbes*, *The Dr. Oz Show*, and *Huffington Post* are a few of the media outlets that have turned to Kay to understand, and educate families, caregivers, and retirees on, this issue.

Both of Kay's parents were diagnosed with moderate stages of dementia in 2012. While she held their durable power of attorney, not every institution recognized it, and in some cases, it took weeks to months to have it recognized so she could help her parents pay their bills, manage their household, and serve as their medical advocate. Kay was raising two children, and both she and her husband held full-time jobs. Managing tasks for her parents was overwhelming, so she created a binder-based system to document, organize, and support them. Many friends and colleagues knew what Kay was going through, and when they started to face similar situations and asked her for a copy of her workbook, MemoryBanc was born.

Kay expected that caregivers would be her biggest clients but instead found that most of her clients were between 40 and 60 years old and purchased the workbook to organize themselves. Today, the tool is primarily used by couples as a way to share information about the tasks they have been dividing and conquering for years. Not only does it offer a simple way to track and organize a household, but it also allows couples to work together in managing shared lives.

AARP Foundation named MemoryBanc an "Older-Adult Focused Innovation."

Acknowledgments

Special thanks to two women who helped give flight to MemoryBanc: Kathy Heiberg and Lynda Alicudo.

There are many along the way who helped me build and focus my vision: Steve Sobel and Brielle Danese helped me craft my business plan and refine my focus. Bob Smith stepped in to help mentor me through the first big steps in growing a sustainable company. The George Washington University and the director of the GW Business Plan Competition, John Rollins, encouraged me and helped refine the MemoryBanc business model.

To Jodi Lipson, a big thank you for reviewing the workbook and helping me bring it to market. To Debby Englander and Margaret Zelsnack, who helped me elevate the workbook editorially, and to Paul McCarthy, who helped make the cover match the idea in my head.

A final thanks to several notable experts who took the time to review the workbook: Bart Astor, author of *AARP Roadmap for the Rest of Your Life: Smart Choices About Money, Health, Work, Lifestyle ... and Pursuing Your Dreams*, which should be on the reading list of everyone over the age of 40; Cynthia R. Green, Ph.D., coauthor of *Your Best Brain Ever: A Complete Guide & Workout* and founder of Total Brain Health; Gary R. McClain, Ph.D., founder of Just Got Diagnosed; and Barbara McVicker, host of the PBS special *Stuck in the Middle: Caring for Mom and Dad*, who immediately helped me realize I'm so not alone on my journey.

MemoryBanc®

≫ ≫ MemoryBanc Workbook
Registration/2015 Order Discount Form

Receive free page downloads, product discounts, and news by registering ownership with MemoryBanc. Respond one of three ways:

1) Visit www.MemoryBanc.com

2) Fax this form to our toll-free fax: 888.841.5234

3) Mail this form to: MemoryBanc, 4601 N. Fairfax Drive, #1200, Arlington, VA 22203

MemoryBanc Workbook	MSRP	Owner Discount	
1 copy	$19.95	$15.96	(20% Off)
2 or more copies	$19.95	$13.97	(Save 30%)

Owner/Purchaser

Name

Address

Phone

Email

Shipping Address (if different):

Name

Address

SHIPPING & HANDLING
If Total < $30.00 $3.50
If Total > $30.00 $6.50

MemoryBanc®

4601 N. Fairfax Drive, Suite 1200
Arlington, VA 22203

Item	Qty	Price	Subtotal
1 Workbook	1	x $15.96 =	
2 or more Workbooks		x $13.97 =	

Total: _____

VA Tax (6%): _____

Shipping & Handling: _____

Order Total: _____

☐ Registration Only

Payment

☐ Charge **Order Total** to Visa/MasterCard/Discover

Credit Card #   Exp. date

Security Code/CVV

Signature

MemoryBanc®

Upgrade to one of these best-selling products:

 **MemoryBanc Register™ Flash Drive Edition**

For individuals desiring a more portable and paperless organization system, our 2 GB flash drive comes preloaded with the MemoryBanc workbook pages in an editable PDF format so you can add, edit, and store your information digitally. Use the 2 GB of space to include estate papers, personal documents, photos—any files you would like to secure. **MSRP $39.95**

MemoryBanc Register Binder Edition

Delivered in a turned and stitched three-ring vegan leather binder with moire lining and front-cover pocket, the preprinted MemoryBanc 8.5 x 11 inch workbook pages with Personal, Financial, Medical, Online, Household, and Other section tabs, make adding pages and updates easy as your information changes, assets grow, and accounts accumulate. Users can tailor this edition to meet specific needs by adding section tabs. All registered owners qualify for FREE refills for life. **MSRP $54.95**

FREE REFILLS FOR LIFE

All registered owners qualify for free annual refills to keep their MemoryBanc Register up to date. A small shipping & handling fee applies.

MemoryBanc Register Combo Edition

Buy the Flash Drive and the Binder together for additional savings and storage options. **MSRP $69.95**

All Upgrades
30% OFF

Expiration Date: 12/31/2015

MemoryBanc

░░░ MemoryBanc 2015 Upgrade Discount Form

Take advantage of our 2015 discount offer by:

1) Visit www.MemoryBanc.com and use coupon code "WORKBOOK"

2) Fax this completed form to our toll-free fax: 888.841.5234

3) Mail this completed form to: MemoryBanc, 4601 N. Fairfax Drive, #1200, Arlington, VA 22203

MemoryBanc Register	MSRP	Owner Discount	
Flash Drive Edition	$39.95	$27.97	(30% Off)
Binder Edition	$54.95	$38.47	(30% Off)
Combo Edition	$69.95	$48.97	(30% Off)

Owner/Purchaser

Name

Address

Phone

Email

Shipping Address (if different):

Name

Address

Item	Qty	Price	Subtotal
Flash Drive Edition		x $27.97 =	
Binder Edition		x $38.47 =	
Combo Edition		x $48.97 =	

Total: _____

VA Tax (6%): _____

Shipping & Handling: $6.50

Order Total: _____

Payment

☐ Charge **Order Total** to Visa/MasterCard/Discover

Credit Card #   Exp. date

Security Code/CVV

Signature

MemoryBanc
4601 N. Fairfax Drive, Suite 1200
Arlington, VA 22203

Printed in the USA
CPSIA information can be obtained
at www.ICGtesting.com
JSHW060041150824
68134JS00028B/2581

9 781630 472498